CONTENTS

An Apostolic People:	3
Part 1:	8
Part 1 (chapters 1-5) explores the following key themes:	9
Introduction	10
Chapter 1:	12
Chapter 2:	19
Chapter 3:	37
Chapter 4:	41
Chapter 5:	46
Part 2:	56
Part 2 (chapters 6-15) explores the following key themes:	58
Chapter 6:	60
Chapter 7:	65
Chapter 8:	69
Chapter 9:	76

Chapter 10:	81
Chapter 11:	85
Chapter 12:	88
Chapter 13:	92
Chapter 14:	99
Chapter 15:	102
Appendix 1:	109
Appendix 2:	122
Appendix 3:	130

AN APOSTOLIC PEOPLE:

FOUNDATIONS AND FEATURES OF AN APOSTOLIC CHURCH

Module Facilitators:

Alistair Matheson & Steven Anderson have both served Christ and His church in Scotland as pastors, apostolic leaders and Bible teachers for more than 30 years.

Alistair currently leads Glasgow City Church and sponsors the Baton Leadership Programme, while Steven, based also at Glasgow City Church, leads the equipping ministry, Kingdom Mentoring.

Module Description

An Apostolic People: Foundations and Features of a Missional Church is a Baton Leadership Programme module designed to lay the biblical foundation of an apostolic church, to examine the leadership gifts through which such a movement is developed and led, and to equip participants to communicate and demonstrate these dynamic features to others. The module incorporates the doctrine of the church as the biblical foundational upon which to develop an understanding of the gifts and graces of Christ that are essential to the mission of an apostolic people. The module combines relevant reading and video resources with the opportunity to write reflectively and engage in stimulating conversation in pastoral supervision meetings.

Objectives

* To provide an understanding of the biblical doctrine of the church.

AN APOSTOLIC PEOPLE

* To provide a biblical understanding of the term 'apostolic' and what it means to be an apostolic people.

* To understand the values which motivate and guide apostolic leaders and communities.

* To recognise the attributes and function of the ministries given by Christ to equip an apostolic movement.

* To equip participants to communicate, inspire and lead local churches towards the fullness of their apostolic commission.

Module Reading:

* Snyder, Howard A. (2004), *The Community of the King*, Inter-Varsity Press, ISBN: 9780830827497

* Cannistraci, David (1996), *Apostles and the Emerging Apostolic Movement: A biblical outlook at apostleship and how God is using it to bless His church today*, Regal Books, ISBN: 978-083072338

* *The Holy Bible.* In Old Testament Survey, it is recommended that you use as your primary text a literal translation (e.g. English Standard Version, New American Standard Bible, King James Version etc.), although dynamic equivalent translations (e.g. New International Version, Good News Bible etc.) and paraphrases (e.g. The Message, The Living Bible etc.) are also useful for reference. For free access to current Bible versions, see: www.biblegateway.com

* *New Bible Dictionary – Third Edition*, Millard, A. R. et al. (1996), Leicester: Inter-Varsity Press, ISBN 0-85110-659-5. Excellent resource for biblical background knowledge.

Study

Manageable weekly study times are important, not only because they alleviate pressure at the assessment stages, but because they instil a disciplined study habit, enable better learning and ensure greater long-term retention of material covered; ultimately, the goal is that you carry the same study habits beyond the Baton Leadership Programme and into lifelong Christian learning.

For your personal study, key reflective questions have been set throughout the module, and it is recommended that you use these for both personal enrichment and future application through your ministry.

Assessment

An Apostolic Church assessment is two-pronged: periodic Supervisor Appointments and a summative essay assignment.

1) Supervisor Appointments. Over the course of the module you will have three meetings with your supervisor. You will be equipped for these discussions by the reflective questions which you will find in this study guide, providing the opportunity

to continuously demonstrate effective engagement with course material. After the final appointment your supervisor will submit a Supervision Form to the Baton Management Team confirming that you have achieved the specified Supervision Appointment outcomes. As your supervisor may also have to schedule appointments with other participants around the same time, please ensure that a mutually convenient date and venue for your first appointment has been arranged as soon as possible, and that you do not leave Supervisor Appointments without having set a date for the next one.

2) Summative Essay Assignment. Your final assessment will consist of the 2,000-3,000 word written assignment as detailed at the end of this plan. This assignment should be submitted to your supervisor at least one week in advance of your third and final supervision appointment and, from there, forwarded to Baton Administration for assessment.

PART 1:

THE FOUNDATION OF AN APOSTOLIC PEOPLE – REVELATION OF THE CHURCH

PART 1 (CHAPTERS 1-5) EXPLORES THE FOLLOWING KEY THEMES:

1. What is church?

2. Ekklesia

3. Cosmic Purpose of the Church

4. Church and Kingdom

5. The Ascended Christ and His Church

INTRODUCTION

The church of Jesus Christ finds its fulfilment as an apostolic people.

The Greek word for 'church', *ekklesia*, means 'called out', while the word for 'apostolic' is *apostolos*, 'sent out'.

It is not an over-simplification to say that we, the church of Jesus Christ, are *called out to be sent out*, a people with a mission to the world that flows from encounter with Christ. We have been commissioned by the Sent One Himself as His ambassadors on earth, continuing the mission which He come into the world to launch and now directs from Heaven.

We have been commissioned by the One who said, *"As the Father sent Me, so I send you."* (John 20:21) To accomplish this, He poured out upon His church at Pentecost the same Holy Spirit who descended upon Him at the commencement of His own earthly ministry, thus enabling us to be and to act like Him on earth.

The goal of this module, *An Apostolic People*, is to discover what a community that is the embodiment of Christ's person and the conduit for His work should look like.

The church, as we shall see, is birthed and grows organically before it becomes structured organisationally; it operates effectively not as an institution but as a movement, inspired by biblical revelation, functioning through spiritual relationship, and governed by flexible structures that serve the life of a growing body.

But let us begin this module but laying the spiritual foundation of that great people against which Christ Jesus Himself said the gates of hell would not prevail: the church.

Our *mission* is really exciting, but perhaps even more wonderful, and fundamental to all we *do*, is what we *are*.

We are *church*!

There is so, so much to unpack.

In *An Apostolic People*, we will at least make a start!

CHAPTER 1:

WHAT IS CHURCH?

Matthew 16:13-20 (NASB): *"Now when Jesus came into the district of Caesarea Philippi, He was asking His disciples, 'Who do people say that the Son of Man is?' And they said, 'Some say John the Baptist; and others, Elijah; but still others, Jeremiah, or one of the prophets.' He said to them, 'But who do you say that I am?' Simon Peter answered, 'You are the Christ, the Son of the living God.' And Jesus said to him, 'Blessed are you, Simon Bar-jona, because flesh and blood did not reveal this to you, but My Father who is in heaven. I also say to you that you are Peter, and upon this rock I will build My church; and the gates of Hades will not overpower it. I will give you the keys of the kingdom of heaven; and whatever you bind on earth shall have been bound in heaven, and whatever you loose on earth shall have been loosed in heaven.' Then He warned the disciples that they should tell no one that He was the Christ."*

Ephesians 5 (NASB): *"Husbands, love your wives, just as Christ also loved the church and gave Himself up for her, so that He might sanctify her, having cleansed her by the washing of water with the word, that He might present to Himself the church in all her glory, having no spot or wrinkle or any such thing; but that she would be holy and blameless."*

Place these two golden passages side by side and you have a composition of revelation and passion that elevates the mind and grips the heart.

Before we elaborate on the doctrine of the church, may I, as module facilitator, clearly and unashamedly reveal my heart.

I do not just believe in the church.

I love the church.

Why?

Because I love Jesus. And loving Jesus, I find myself

loving what Jesus loves. And He loves nothing more than the church. *His* church. The chosen people He died for and ever lives for.

Warts, blemishes and all. Contradictions, offences, short-comings, hypocrisies, foibles and failings. Every reason some people have to walk away from church, justifies the resolve of Christ to cleanse and purify, to mature and exhort, to build up and perfect.

Let me be honest. I thank God for the times Jesus didn't walk away from me. I am more grateful than I can express for the times He could have left my church, too, but did not. That has proven to be one of the primary differences between Jesus and some Christians!

I will never forget the time a loved and trusted friend walked up to me just as I was about to open a Sunday morning service, placed in my hand the keys of the facility where our church plant met, looked at me pitifully and blurted, "I'm leaving this church; it's never going to grow." I never saw him in our church again.

But Jesus kept coming.

And, despite what would have been a variety of other justifiable reasons to leave us too, Jesus just kept on coming back. He kept coming until we started to grow. I've moved on now, but they're still growing. In fact, they've only gone and planted another church since I left. Jesus is still there. Still loving them, working with them, changing them. Still growing them.

Is this not the nature of church?

Church is more than a doctrine, glorious though that doctrine is. Church is the object of Christ's undying, unstoppable love.

He loves His church and has already demonstrated to it commitment beyond death.

Jesus wonderfully revealed Himself to me, entered my life and gave me His Holy Spirit at four o-clock in the morning on Saturday 6th February, 1982 and, ever since then, I have loved Him. I consider my entire life an offering of thanks for what He has done for me and for those I am now blessed to call my children.

My love for Jesus cannot be expressed in any more obvious and direct way than by loving His church. It is because love for Jesus and love for His church are absolutely inseparable that, speaking to Peter, Christ Himself accompanied the question, *"Do you love Me?"* with the command, *"Tend My flock."*

To love Jesus is to serve His people.

If Jesus loves the church, so must I. When I share the cup of Communion, my covenant with Jesus extends to the community which is betrothed to Him.

For better, for worse. For richer, for poorer. In sickness and in health – but never to be parted by death.

I have never been fooled by those who say they love Christ but have no time for church. They do not love the real Jesus. They cannot know Him. They certainly do not follow Him. Jesus goes to church. He comes to my local church every time we meet. To use loftier, biblical language, the people of Christ are His place of abiding, the temple of His presence, 'the dwelling of God in the Spirit'.

Let's unpack a little more.

Because Christ is protective of His church, I am protective of it too. My own wonderful wife may not be perfect, but let no one speak disrespectfully or destructively of her in my presence! If they do, they should not be surprised if my defensive instincts are aroused!

It is no different with the church. When people speak against church – any church where Christ is loved and His Gospel preached – I take it personally. It is something I take to heart, not merely a cerebral or philosophical matter.

Every Christian should have this instinctive protectiveness for the church, not just their local expression, but the entire body of Christ. Paul emphasised to the Corinthians that when one part of the body suffers the whole body suffers with it. As the late Ern Baxter once quipped in poetic humour, "A pain in the head puts the whole body to bed!"

I am always in some way diminished by the disappointments of other Christians, and always enlarged by their successes and victories, no matter who or where they are. It doesn't matter how distant another Christian movement may seem to be, I am affected by its joys and sorrows. Whoever my brothers and sisters may be, I am of the same blood. Much though my Jesus loves me, He loves them no less. Disparage them and you disparage me.

This is the nature of the church as one body.

As Paul wrote to the Ephesians (4:4-6, NASB), *"There is one body and one Spirit, just as also you were called in one hope of your calling; one Lord, one faith, one baptism, one God and Father of all who is over all and through all and in all."*

These statements are much more than sentiment. Neither are they are not about unity for unity's sake, but for Christ's sake. When Jesus prayed that His people might be one, He was not blinded by emotion, all heat and no light. His intercession was fired by a vision of one people who would, with one voice, declare and display His plan of redemption to all creation. His was an enlightened passion, an intelligent flame.

Alluding to the apostle Paul's teaching on the

church, Howard Snyder describes us as *"nothing less than the body of no one less than Jesus Christ."* (Snyder, 2010) But Paul's own language is even more dramatic: the church, he declares, is *"the fulness of Him who fills all in all."* (Ephesians 1:23, NASB)

Talking of language, where does the word *church* come from, and what does it mean?

CHAPTER 2:

EKKLESIA

Etymology

The Greek word translated church in the New Testament is *ekklesia*, derived from *ek* (out) and *klesia* (called). So the New Testament church, from the outset, was understood to be the company of 'called out ones.'

The English and Scots words 'church' and 'kirk' are well intended terms but not the most accurate translations of *ekklesia*. The old English 'circe' is derived from the Greek *kuriakos*, which literally translates as "The Lord's". Few would argue that the church is the Lord's, but *kuriakos* appears only twice in the New Testament (I Corinthians 11:20; Revelation 1:10) and it reveals little about the origin, nature and purpose of *ekklesia*, the word for the community which Christ said the gates of hell would not prevail against (Matthew 16:18). The Scottish Gaelic word *eaglais* and the French *église* are much truer to the Greek text than the English word *church* is. In English, the scholarly terms 'ecclesiology' and 'ecclesiastical' are back on the right track, even if understandably a bit stuffy for common usage!

How was ekklesia used in ancient Greece?

The *ekklesia* was the principal assembly of the democracy of ancient Athens (C5th BC), which would convene up to four times a month and was responsible for important decisions, such as declaring wars or electing politicians and generals. The spontaneous assembly *(ekklesia)* that convened at Ephesus in Acts chapter 19 for a town council-type public gathering was typical of the term's secular usage by the time the New Testament was written ...

> "The city was filled with the confusion, and they rushed with one accord into the theatre, dragging along Gaius and Aristarchus, Paul's traveling companions from Macedonia. And

when Paul wanted to go into the assembly, the disciples would not let him. Also some of the Asiarchs who were friends of his sent to him and repeatedly urged him not to venture into the theatre. So then, some were shouting one thing and some another, for the assembly [ekklesia] *was in confusion and the majority did not know for what reason they had come together. Some of the crowd concluded it was Alexander, since the Jews had put him forward; and having motioned with his hand, Alexander was intending to make a defence to the assembly. But when they recognised that he was a Jew, a single outcry arose from them all as they shouted for about two hours, 'Great is Artemis of the Ephesians!' After quieting the crowd, the town clerk said, 'Men of Ephesus, what man is there after all who does not know that the city of the Ephesians is guardian of the temple of the great Artemis and of the image which fell down from heaven? So, since these are undeniable facts, you ought to keep calm and to do nothing rash. For you have brought these men here who are neither robbers of temples nor blasphemers of our goddess. So then, if Demetrius and the craftsmen who are with him have a complaint against any man, the courts are in session and proconsuls are available; let them bring charges against one another. But if you want anything beyond this, it shall be settled in the lawful assembly* [ekklesia]. *For indeed we are in danger of being accused of a riot in connection with today's events, since there is no real cause for it, and in this connection we will be unable to account for this disorderly gathering.' After saying this he dismissed the assembly* [ekklesia]."

Acts 19:29-41, NASB

How did Jewish people understand ekklesia in New Testament times?

In a religious context, the courts of the Jews exercised similar powers to the Greek assembly in and before the time of Christ. The rabbinical practice of 'binding and loosing' (forbidding and permitting) was exercised in this forum. Interestingly, Christ Himself appeared to boldly practise His own powers of binding and loosing, something that no doubt contributed to the growing resentment of the Jews as their established institutions increasingly felt threatened by His spiritual authority. For example, in the Sermon on the Mount Jesus repeatedly declared, *"You have heard that it was said ... but I say to you ..."* (Matthew 5, NASB), upgrading existing laws to a higher, internalised standard based on heart attitude.

Later in Matthew's Gospel (– see 16:19 and 18:18), Jesus went on to delegate powers of binding and loosing to Simon Peter and His new *ekklesia* for matters of church governance. Such powers were later put to work in instances such as the Acts 15 directive by the apostles and elders regarding Gentile circumcision and the law of Moses, issuing a ruling that *"seemed good to the Holy Spirit and to us"* (verse 28). These powers of binding and loosing might also be assumed in Paul's advice to the Corinthians to form their own church courts, rather than turning to civil law, to resolve internal disputes (– see I Cor. 6:1-9).

Understood against such contexts, *ekklesia* might be understood as a body of people called together out of the world, under Christ's authority, to discern God's will for church matters and to participate in His strategy for extending His kingdom on earth.

Did ekklesia exist in the Old Testament?

Matthew's Gospel has been referred to as the 'Gospel of the Church' because it is the only Gospel, and the first book in the New Testament, to teach about *ekklesia*, a doctrine that came first from the lips of Christ Himself. But Matthew's Gospel is not really the first place in the Bible where the idea of *ekklesia* is to be found.

The Septuagint, sometimes abbreviated as 'LXX' (70), was a translation of the Hebrew Scriptures into Koine Greek in the 3rd century BC by a group of seventy Jewish scholars. The LXX uses *ekklesia* on numerous occasions to translate the Hebrew 'qahal', which English translations commonly render 'assembly' or 'congregation' in our Old Testaments. Qahal is derived from qol, the word for 'voice', and refers to the summoning of an assembly, in a similar way to what is understood by *ekklesia*, 'called out'. New Testament writers would have been very familiar with the Septuagint usage of *ekklesia*.

Here are some of many examples of *ekklesia* in the Septuagint translation of the Old Testament:

> "... Then Moses spoke in the hearing of all the assembly [ekklesia] of Israel the words of this song..." (Deuteronomy. 31:30)

> "... That all this assembly [ekklesia] may know that the Lord does not deliver by sword or by spear ..." (I Samuel 17:47)

> "... Sing to the Lord a new song, and His praise in the congregation [ekklesia] of the godly ones ..." (Psalm 149:1)

It is consistent with the teaching ministry of Jesus to use common language and imagery with which

His hearers were already well familiar to illustrate the truths He preached, and so we should not be surprised to learn that *ekklesia* was far from a new concept to the Jewish audience of His day.

Ekklesia in the Gospels

Therefore, when Jesus declared, *"I will build My church!"* (Matthew 16:18), rather than inventing some revolutionary new idea, He was taking personal possession of an age-old term and re-energising it with new meaning, purpose and scope.

Jesus lifted the concept of church to a new level. Just as He brought in a 'new law' in the Sermon on the Mount (Matthew 5-7), cleaned up His Father's house by driving the money-changers out of the temple (John 2:13-16), upstaged the high priest on the last day of the feast by heralding a coming generation of Spirit-filled people (John 7:37-39), superseded Passover with The Lord's Supper (Matthew 26:26-28) and so on, Jesus effectively took over, elevated and re-branded the term *ekklesia*.

A new nation

Jesus' purpose was to call out a new congregation, a community spiritually authorised and empowered in a manner never before experienced by any people on earth, populated by Jew and Gentile without distinction, a 'new nation' over whom He would be King, Head and Shepherd. This New Testament *ekklesia*, as we shall see, is something more glorious than a 'new improved version' of the old. Although Jesus only explicitly mentions *ekklesia* twice in the Gospels (Matthew 16:13-20, 18:15-20), it is quite clear that He has come to establish something radically new. The other Gospels may not use the term *ekklesia*, but its presence is not difficult to find.

Shepherd and flock

For example, in John chapter 10, the Shepherd comes to God's flock and calls them out – *"... the sheep hear his voice, and he calls his own sheep by name and leads them out ..."* (verse 3, NASB) – to be an outward moving people who would no longer draw security from the familiarity of their place of waiting, but from following within obedient ear-shot of the Good Shepherd's voice – *"... My sheep hear My voice, and I know them and they follow Me; ... and no one will snatch them out of My hand."* (verses 27-28, NASB) Indeed, wherever Jesus issued the call, 'Follow Me!' He was effectively inviting people to join His called out company, the growing assembly that would become recognised as the church.

Ekklesia **in the New Testament**

A popular evangelical position is that the church was birthed at Pentecost although some, such as notable preacher and author, the late Martin Lloyd-Jones, have held the view that Pentecost was not the beginning of the church but the empowering of an already existing church. In *Joy Unspeakable*, Lloyd-Jones suggested that the church may actually have been constituted when the resurrected Jesus breathed the Holy Spirit upon His disciples (John 20:21-23). At whatever moment it was actually birthed on earth, the church of Jesus Christ, as we now know it, although it traces some of its most visible forms and practices back to the Jewish synagogue, is a New Testament creation and revelation, led by the ascended Christ, empowered by the promised and outpoured Holy Spirit and equipped by God's gifts and graces, the earthly representation of Christ who is Himself the perfect embodiment of the Triune God.

The church cannot now be identified apart from Jesus Christ, who is *"... Head of the body, the church* [ekklesia]; ... *the beginning, the firstborn from the dead, so that He Himself will come to have first place in everything."* (Colossians 1:18, NASB)

The temple of God

The New Testament church, as *"a dwelling of God in the Spirit"* (Ephesians 2:22, NASB), *"a spiritual house for a holy priesthood"* (1 Pet. 2:5, NASB), is something much greater than a continuation of or even improvement on the Old Testament flock; it is the place of the holy presence of God, more akin to the Old Testament temple. The congregation of Israel were represented before God in tabernacle and temple; the New Testament church *became* the temple themselves, the dwelling where God permanently abides on earth! Ideas of sacred buildings, places of pilgrimage and mediators between men and God (other than Christ Himself) are obsolete for a people who have themselves *become* the sacred place!

How can anyone who apprehends such wonderful truth, and who claims to love and believe in Christ, possibly fail to love and believe in the church?! God and His church are not to be found in different places. When I hear of seekers abandoning the fellowship of *ekklesia* to go sailing or climb mountains in order to 'feel near to God', I ask, 'Which god is that?' Of course, the earth and stars are God's handiwork and reflect untold wonders of his being, and who can fail to be enthralled by the wonderful animal kingdom of David Attenborough's documentaries?!

But *ekklesia* is what He calls home, the place where He best and most easily reveals Himself on earth.

Ephesians – 'Epistle of the Church'

It is upon the New Testament revelation and reality of Christ Jesus Himself that the community of Christian believers, the church, is now built. And it is within this church that the scriptures teach us how to live. No understanding of the church is complete without a detailed study of the 'twin epistles' of Ephesians and Colossians, letters that gloriously partner to paint a masterpiece of the union of the pre-eminent Head, Jesus Christ, with His chosen body of people. Ephesians is frequently referred to as 'the epistle of the church' because here we discover wonderful truths about the church's position, nature, identity, purpose and strategy. As the body of Christ, the church is to be understood as the expression of Christ's person and plan, not just for mankind but for absolutely everything else too! The church is God's building, His base of redemptive operation, place of spiritual dwelling and so much more.

Unfortunately, down through the centuries, as happens with all words in all languages, 'church' has accumulated baggage and, by association and connotation, assumed many extra meanings with which we shall not be too concerned here. While there is an obvious place for the useful 'wineskins', containers in time and place, we shall not, for example, focus on dictionary definitions of church such as buildings, denominations, Sunday services and so on, things that are not identified as *ekklesia* in the New Testament.

How, then, should we define 'church'?

Reflective Question:

2.1. In what ways is the study of 'ekklesia' enhancing you understanding of what Church is?

Definition of 'Church'

Howard Snyder (2010) reduces his definition of church to five words: *"the community of God's people."* (*The Community of the King, p. 74*). For him, this definition encapsulates the two key elements of 'people-hood' (or race and kingdom identity) and 'community' (or fellowship and corporate life).

The New Testament allows room for only two understandings of the church: the universal church and the local church.

The universal church

The universal church is understood by most scholars as the company of all believers of all time. Such a definition includes all those who lived and believed before Christ, although these did not experience the benefits of Christ's church in their own lifetime. They include our *"great cloud of witnesses"* (Hebrews 12:1), not least *"Abraham, who is the father of us all"* (Romans 4:16), who *"rejoiced to see [Jesus'] day"* (John 8:56). These Old Testament role models of faith lived in anticipation of something greater, receiving God's promises and welcoming them from a distance (Hebrews 11:13), and would one day be *"made perfect"* together with us (Hebrews 11:40), in what we now refer to as the universal church of Jesus Christ.

The local church

The local church is any group of believers which meets regularly in a given location in the belief that *"... where two or three have gathered together in My name, I am there in their midst."* (Matthew 18:20) But such congregations are more than an informal 'getting together'; the local church is marked by mutual, inter-dependent relationship under Christ and accompanied in the New Testament by *"... the apostles' teaching, ... fellowship, ... the breaking of bread and ... prayer."* (Acts 2:42) Membership of this Church in the Book of Acts is entered into through profession of faith and baptism (Acts 2:41).

The Identity of the Church

Before moving onto the purpose of the church, it is worth dwelling on some of the beautiful metaphors used in the New Testament to describe it.

Each of numerous metaphors reveals special features of the church. For example, the church is described as a pastured flock (John 10:1-18; also developed in Hebrews 13:20-21 and I Peter 5:2-4), a cultivated vine (John 15:1-11), a planting and a field (I Corinthians 3:6-9), a household (Galatians 6:10), a bride (Ephesians 5:22-23), a pillar and support of the truth (I Timothy 3:15), and a royal priesthood (I Peter 2:5-9).

Two of the most commonly used metaphors for the church already alluded to, used by Paul with the Ephesians, are significant in that they describe the church both *organically* and *organisationally (structurally)*.

The Church as a Body

See Ephesians 1:22-23; 2:15-16; 4:4, 11-16.

Body conveys the idea of organic life. This analogy is developed in much more detail in I Corinthians 12, but it is also used repeatedly in Ephesians. As with any organism, growth and reproduction are natural and inevitable consequences of life (Note: the church in the Book of Acts and historically since then is marked by three dimensions of growth:

spiritual, numerical and geographical). Snyder emphasises that the church should be understood primarily as an organism rather than a structure, a charismatic community rather than an institution. Of course, the growth of any organism is not chaotic or haphazard, but is governed by natural laws and is remarkably patterned. But the organisational must always serve, never confine or restrict, the organic.

The Church as a Building (or Temple)

See Ephesians 2:19-22

Here, the church can be seen as an organisation. But we must be careful with this metaphor because, as Peter emphasised (I Peter 2:4-8), we are talking here about a temple of *"living"* stones. This speaks of a structure that is flexible and Snyder stresses: *"All biblical figures for the church suggest a charismatic and organic, rather than an institutional, model; tree, vine, flock, family, nation, household and even the living and growing 'holy temple' (Ephesians 2:21)"* (p. 84). While Snyder says it would be naive to pretend the church is not an institution, and misguided to suggest that some elements of institution are not necessary or even desirable, he and many others have used Jesus' parable of the wineskins (Matthew 9:17) to warn of the dangers of institutionalisation.

Structure that serves life

Nevertheless, 'building' creates an image of stability and permanence, symmetry and order. It was not long before the phenomenal organic growth of the church of Acts was met by the need for order through the setting in place of deacons (6:1-6). This introduction of structure was immediately justified by subsequent and continued organic growth (6:7). Similarly, Paul's appeal for good governance at Corinth (see I Corinthians 14) was necessary to protect, not stifle, their spiritual gifts (See I Corinthians 12). The priority is clear: structure and government, though essential, are there to protect and enhance life and growth, but the organism must always take priority over the organisation.

Dangers of age

The church as an institution should always be able to recognise, accommodate and release gifting and potential, but an institution can never *create* these; they are dynamic effects of Christ at work in His church through His Spirit and word, bringing about His plan through individuals and communities as they respond to divine calling and eternal purpose. When an institution ages and becomes rigid, Snyder says, it will periodically need to undergo renewal and reformation, if it is to accommodate new growth. Such changes can be difficult and painful. But then, with a healthy exercise programme in place, rigidity need not accompany age! Surely it is easier to maintain a flexible posture of lifelong development than, having settled for what we have and stiffening into modes of preservation and maintenance, to rejuvenate and transition for growth? Discipleship and change should never cease for the Christian community, and the nature of *church* is that spiritual growth is as much a collective experience as it is individual.

Contemporary dangers

And so Snyder suggests a contemporary threat to organic church life is reliance on modern secular institutional structures: "*The tendency to build large local churches, with the accompanying inevitable institutionalism, bureaucracy and emphasis on buildings, is too easy. The subtle temptation to imitate secular models such as government, the shopping mall and the university becomes overwhelming, and the church slips into institutionalism, with the rigidity, impersonality and hierarchy that go along with the pattern.*" (The Community of the King, *p.* 144)

Beware!

The purpose of this module, *An Apostolic People*, is to ensure that, by intentionally maintaining a clear sense of mission, vision, cultural values and strategy, our local churches never become disconnected from the pristine purpose that keeps us living and growing, not just organically but also organisationally.

Reflective Questions:

2.2.1. How effectively is your local church 'staying fresh'?

2.2.2. How are churches and individual Christians to be saved from slipping from mission to duty, from dynamic life into institutional maintenance?

CHAPTER 3:

COSMIC PURPOSE OF THE CHURCH

Snyder speaks of a 'cosmic' purpose as something that is greater and farther reaching than the saving of souls, essential and central though that is. *"Redemption,"* he says, *"is the centre of God's plan, but it is not the circumference of that plan."* God's plan of reconciliation, according to the apostle Paul, involves *"... the summing up of all things in Christ, things in the heavens and things on the earth, things in the heavens and things on the earth."* (Ephesians 1:10, NASB). What begins with personal salvation (Ephesians 2:8-9) leads to *"good works ... prepared beforehand"* (2:10); works that are a demonstration of *"the manifold (or, multi-coloured) wisdom of God ... through the church to the rulers and the authorities in the heavenly places."* (3:10).

The master plan

The Fall of Man began with Adam's sin breaking not just his own, but mankind's, fellowship with God. The effects of this breach extended far beyond Adam's fractured relationship with God. The results of sin were cosmic in scope, resulting in psychological, physical, social, political and environmental destruction and decay. When Adam and Eve sinned, they took the planet with them, bringing creation into subservience to the 'god of this world', Satan, and his spiritual principalities and powers.

God's plan of redemption

But Christ, the 'second Adam', came to reconcile man to God and to reverse the effects of the Fall. As with the Fall, redemption begins but does not stop with bridging the spiritual gap between God and man. God's plan of reconciliation was to redeem not just man but all of His creation from the results of sin, whether psychological, physical, social, political or environmental. In short, everything affected by the sin and fall of Adam was to become subject to the righteousness and reconciliation of Christ. According to Paul, the whole of creation *"groans"* (See Romans 8:18-25), longing for a coming age when the great master plan that begins with the salvation of sinners finally sets His creation free from its slavery to the corruption of the Fall.

Which brings us to the great purpose of the Church: to manifest Christ's intention as *"head over all things to the church"* (Ephesians 1:22, NASB); to demonstrate God's master plan to reconcile all things – beginning with man but extending to all creation – to Himself and to bring every spiritual principality and power under subjection to Jesus Christ. The church, *"seated ... with Him in the heavenly places,"* (Ephesians 2:6, NASB) has been *"created in Christ Jesus"* (Ephesians 2:10, NASB) with this glorious *"administration"* (Ephesians 1:10, NASB) in mind.

The 'theocratic' strategy (See Part 2, Section 10:

Apostolic Values) of Ephesians reveals that, in order to achieve the all-encompassing purpose of Christ for His church, the ascended Christ has granted enabling gifts, transmitted directly from the Heavenly Head to His body on earth by the Holy Spirit. These gifts, found in Ephesians chapter 4, are sometimes referred to as the 'fivefold' or 'ascension' ministries and will be examined in Part 2 of this module. These ministries are not an end in themselves, but simply a means to the much greater end of maturing and mobilising a glorious church for the fulness of Christ's expression.

But before we look further at the church, something should be understood regarding the nature of the kingdom of God, without which it is not possible to properly understand the purpose and role of the church. Snyder does this topic great justice in *The Community of the King* – an extremely relevant and useful work – and certain points he makes should be particularly emphasised.

CHAPTER 4:

CHURCH AND KINGDOM

Firstly, what is the kingdom of God?

For the Christian, the kingdom of God is the place where Christ reigns as King, and that kingdom is established wherever His will is invoked. This is the first appeal of The Lord's Prayer: *"Your kingdom come! Your will be done on earth, as it is in heaven!"*

As Paul taught the Romans, the rule of Christ is one of righteousness: *"The kingdom of God is ... righteousness and peace and joy in the Holy Spirit."* (Romans 14:17) Paul had begun this epistle by declaring that through the Gospel the *"righteousness of God is revealed."* (Romans 1:17) This is the same *"gospel of the kingdom"* (Matthew 24:14 and elsewhere) spoken of by Jesus. Christ poignantly coupled His kingdom and righteousness when He urged, *"... Seek first His kingdom and His righteousness ..."* (Matthew 6:33)

Jesus excluded mere lip service from the kingdom of God with the rhetorical question, *"Why do you call Me, 'Lord, Lord,' and do not do what I say?"* (Luke 6:46) These words were a prelude to His teaching about a house that is built upon a rock-solid foundation by hearing His words and acting upon them. Christ's kingdom rule alone, as revealed through the gospel message which some Hebrew believers were later tempted to turn away from, is the *"kingdom which cannot be shaken."* (Hebrews 12:28)

Secondly, how does the church relate to the kingdom?

This brings us to the relationship between the kingdom and the church. Christ and His kingdom are the rock upon which the church is built, and against which *"the gates of hell shall not prevail."* (Matthew 16:18, KJV) The church is not the kingdom, but it is where the kingdom of God is to be found. In fact, the church's identity, health and growth are so dependent upon the kingdom of God that, when it loses its grip on the kingdom of God and vice versa, it ceases to be church. This is why we cannot define the church without understanding the kingdom.

The church, in a very real sense, is the embassy of the kingdom of God on earth, the place where the righteous culture of heaven is to be found, written in the lives of human 'epistles', the 'foreigners' spoken of by Peter when he wrote, *"Keep your behaviour excellent among the Gentiles, so that in the thing in which they slander you as evildoers, they may because of your good deeds, as they observe them, glorify God in the day of visitation."* (I Peter 2:12, NASB)

Church as Agent of the Kingdom of God

Snyder describes the church as *"the agent of the kingdom of God"*, the people through which the rule of

Jesus Christ is to be expressed. But, like any sound biblical scholar, Snyder also urges a balanced position regarding the kingdom (*The Community of the King*, pp. 28-32), issuing a warning relating to two opposing imbalances.

In short, on one hand there is the 'kingdom *now*' position, often associated with a postmillennialist view that the kingdom of God is to be fully established on earth by the church before the return of Christ, which can dilute to a merely 'social gospel', where Christians become so engaged in every area of improving society that they neglect to preach the gospel message that encapsulates the Christ-exalting purpose of everything the church is and does. On the other hand is the 'kingdom *then*' position, often associated with a premillennialist view that the world is going to get worse and worse, with the church as a surviving remnant until the return of Christ, which can lead to a pessimistic view of social engagement and a mentality of 'the worse it gets, the better it is,' where the church huddles away to the point of irrelevance.

A balanced view

Because the kingdom of God has come, is coming and will come, and since the church is the agency of God's kingdom on earth, the healthiest position is to be found somewhere between the above two extremes. The Christian church must preach the new birth as the point of entry to the kingdom of God but, as salt and light in the world, it should also demonstrate and declare biblical standards within every culture and in all institutions of public life, and should do so explicitly in the name of our King, Jesus Christ.

With this brief introduction to the underpinning nature of the kingdom of God to everything the church is and does, we are better equipped to return to the grand strategy of the Book of Ephesians, by which the church is to reveal its ascended King and Head, Jesus Christ, and demonstrate His redemptive plan to all creation, *"things in the heavens, and things on the earth."* (Ephesians 1:10)

Reflective Question:

4. How might the relationship between church and kingdom best be understood and described?

CHAPTER 5:

THE ASCENDED CHRIST AND HIS CHURCH

As alluded to earlier, we see repeatedly in Colossians and Ephesians the inseparable nature of Christ and His church. Christ, writes Paul, is *"head over all things to the church, which is His body, the fulness of Him who fills all in all."* (Ephesians 1:22-23, NASB) As Head of the body, Jesus Christ wills to express the fullness of His person and ministry through an equipped church, a united body that collectively amounts to *"a mature man."* (Ephesians 4:13, NASB).

The narrative of Christ in the Gospels is reproduced in the Book of Acts by a Spirit-filled church, with the ascended Christ now directing affairs from the *"right hand of God"* in heaven (Acts 7:56). A full expression of the same Jesus, by the power of the same Holy Spirit who was once sent by the Father upon the Son, but has now been sent by the Son upon His church. Pointing to the time of His future ascension, Christ had promised, *"The works that I do, [the believer] will do also; and greater works than these he will do; because I go to the Father."* (John 14:12, NASB)

What was Christ's earthly ministry?

Jesus was God's Apostle, sent as the divine ambassador of God's kingdom on earth, establishing what would come to be known as the church, a 'new nation' drawn from all tribes and tongues. He was The Prophet who revealed God to the people, showing them where they truly were, and pointing all who would hear toward what lay up ahead. He was God's Evangelist, preaching a message of repentance and salvation to all who would believe, confirmed by gracious displays of mercy and of power. Jesus was God's Pastor, the Good Shepherd who prepares a table of nurture and leads His flock in secure paths in the midst of life's greatest challenges. Jesus was The Teacher whose irrefutable wisdom and eternal truths provided a foundation to outlast every passing storm.

So, when the soon-to-be-ascended Christ told His apostolic people, *"As the Father has sent* (Greek, *apestelo*) *Me, I also send you,"* (John 20:21) He was preparing them, collectively, to continue and multiply the full expression of His own earthly ministry, to be imparted through the Holy Spirit, descending from heaven on the church, just as He had alighted on Christ as a dove at His baptism in the Jordan. Just as the mantle of Elijah mantle fell to be taken up by Elisha, so the clothing of power on Jesus, ministry was handed down to the church on the Day of Pentecost. In Ephesians chapter 4:8, 11-13 (NASB) we read,

> *"When He ascended on high, ... He gave gifts to men, ... and He gave some as apostles, and some as prophets, and some as evangelists, and some as pastors and teachers, for the equipping of the saints for the work of service, to the building up of the body of Christ; until we all attain to the unity of the faith, and of the knowledge of the Son of God, to a mature man, to the measure of the stature which belongs to the fulness of Christ."*

These ascension gifts of apostle, prophet, evangelist, pastor and teacher were not given as ends in themselves, but strategic means to the end of equipping, building up and unifying Christ's entire body, the church. It is the full complement of this mature, equipped and diverse-yet-united collective, that alone adds up to the fullness of Christ's expression. Christ Himself had prayed, *"... that they may be perfected [matured] in unity, so that the world may know that You sent Me."* (John 17:23, NASB)

In this module, we shall go on to identify and consider these ministries in detail, but they need to be introduced from the outset as their function is key to understanding the identity, purpose and ministry of the glorious creation that we simply call ... church.

The equipping of the saints

Wherever genuine examples of Christ's ascension ministry gifts have been welcomed in the church, the result has been *"the equipping of the saints"* – the entire church – where *"... the whole body, being fitted and held together by what every joint supplies, according to the proper working of each individual part, causes the growth of the body for the building up of itself in love."* (Ephesians 4:16, NASB)

Where ascension gifts are present, they do not

merely 'do' the ministry; rather, they equip the church to do it. This is a radical concept that has all too rarely been experienced since the Book of Acts, even in many of today's Pentecostal and charismatic churches where, in *theory*, 'body ministry' is normally unquestioningly accepted. Snyder warns against rigid structures that restrict ministry to the few rather than releasing it to the many: "*The clergy-laity split is a direct carryover from pre-Reformation Roman Catholicism and a throwback to the Old Testament priesthood.*" (pp. 112-113)

Reflective Question:

5.1. "Paul's cosmic vision of the church could be summarised as: all of Christ in all the church to all creation."

Briefly, in light of the Ephesians strategy, how would you explain this to a new Christian?

Gifts and Government

Church, as we have seen, is both organism and organisation, life and structure, gifting and government. The dynamic and structural aspects are interdependent, each working to serve the other, but with the clear understanding that the organisational is there to serve and, as necessary, adapt itself to the spiritual, numerical and geographical growth of the organic church.

Elders and Deacons

Ascension ministries are described in Ephesians (4:8, 11) as gifts, sent by Christ to lead and mobilise the entire church for service. But Christ has also set in the local church offices of government – elders and deacons (I Timothy 3:1-13; Titus 1:5-9) – to provide it with the discipline and order necessary to fulfil its mission.

'One man ministry' is alien to the New Testament, whether it is a plurality of elders in the local church or Paul's apostolic teams in itinerant ministry. Whether Paul was being sent out by a team of local leaders in Antioch (Acts 13:1-3) or the collaborative decision making of apostles and elders in Jerusalem in negotiating a potential crisis (Acts 15:1-31), gifted people were always under authority, just as those in governmental office were also dependent on Spirit-anointed input through the giftings of Christ.

Gifting and government together

There is, of course, huge overlap between gifting (abilities) and government (offices); it has been suggested that the lack of reference to 'pastors' in the New Testament may suggest that the term – descriptive of a gifting – was assumed within the role of 'elders' – denoting an office. 'Elder' is primarily a term of seniority with connotations of authority and 'pastor' one of function with allusion to a particular skill-set necessary for the care of the church. It could be assumed that the office of elder should be filled by someone with pastoral capacity, hence the inclusion in Timothy's list of eldership qualifications of the likes of *"hospitable"* and *"peaceable"* (I Timothy 3:2). Note how the apostle John introduces himself as "elder" in his epistles (II John 1; III John 1), referring to his office of oversight as distinct from the capacities, or gifts, such as pastor and teacher, that equipped him for the role.

Just as the office of elder itself requires spiritual gifting to fulfil the role, another example being *"apt to teach"* (I Timothy 3:2), so also the other office of deacon requires its own skill-set also, such as "gifts of helps" (I Corinthians 12:28). With respect to the latter, it should be emphasised that all gifting is 'spiritual', powerfully illustrated by the first deacons (Acts 6:3) who were described as *"full of the Spirit and of wisdom."* (NASB)

Whatever the office or ministry, there is one crucial feature of leadership in the New Testament church, whether locally or 'on the road': it is always marked by team and accountability. Elders are always appointed in a plurality. Apostles always travel in teams and frequently with prophets. There is no such entity as 'the' pastor, other than Christ Himself. This does not mean that there will not be leadership within a team, as seen in the likes of apostles Peter and Paul, but the Spirit-filled church is a body with one head, Jesus Christ – the One who Himself never acts out of union with the Father and the Holy Spirit. In short, there is no biblical warranty for pastors or any other ministers operating outside of submission to a wider eldership team.

A clear understanding of and respect for the interdependence of gifting and government are essential to ensure that, firstly, gifted individuals are accountable to church government, and secondly, church government is influenced and shaped by Christ's gifts. Where spiritual gifting and sound governance are kept in good balance, the church will be healthy.

Full expression of Christ's gifts

An equally importance balance is should be maintained between the local church and the wider body. A local leadership team cannot function effectively outside of healthy, balanced exposure to the full range of ascension ministries through which Christ has chosen to express Himself to the church, some of which, especially apostles, prophets and evangelists, are more likely to operate trans-locally. Where there are limited resources locally, it is essential to the health of any congregation that needed ascension gifts be regularly called in, to enable as complete an expression of Christ as possible.

Where the ministry gifts of Ephesians 4:11-12 and I Corinthians 12:28 are in operation, the church will further be inspired, equipped and released to operate in the manifestation gifts of the Spirit (I Corinthians 12:7-11) and in a diversity of motivational gifts (Romans 12:3-8) (See Part 2, Appendix 3: Prophecy and Prophets in the New Testament), under the guardianship, guidance and service of local church offices of elders and deacons (or whatever terminology a church prefers to use for their necessary functions).

It is in such an environment that the next generation of gifts and callings can be expected to be incubated and hatched to replenish healthy local churches, as 'the whole body' regenerates itself through the Spirit's gifting.

Reflective Questions:

5.2.1. What 'checks and balances' are needed for the growth of a healthy church?

5.2.2. Reflect on different types and levels of gifting described in the following passages of Scripture:

'Manifestation' gifts of I Corinthians 12:4-11, as once-off effects of the Spirit through any Spirit-filled believer; 'Motivational' gifts of Romans 12:3-8, which operate regularly in certain believers; and 'Ministry' gifts, where leaders are gifted to mature and equip the church for the work of the ministry.

5.2.3. What types and levels of gifting have you been conscious of in your life? How have these been remarked upon by others?

PART 2:

THE FEATURES OF AN APOSTOLIC PEOPLE – APOSTOLIC MINISTRY

The following resources should provide a helpful introduction to Part 3 of this module. You may find it helpful to take notes as you listen to the audio file.

Listen:
Apostolic Conversations 1 – An Apostolic People [1]
Phelim Doherty and Steven Anderson with Alistair Matheson; Glasgow, 2020.

PART 2 (CHAPTERS 6-15) EXPLORES THE FOLLOWING KEY THEMES:

6. What is an apostle?

7. Christ our Apostle

8. Ascension gift ministries - overview and purpose

9. What do we mean by 'church'?

10. Church models in Acts

11. Foundation of apostles and prophets

12. Apostolic history - why was apostolic ministry arginalised?

13. Characteristics and functions of apostolic ministry

14. Apostolic teams

15. Being an apostolic people: apostolic culture

CHAPTER 6:

WHAT IS AN APOSTLE?

The following resources should provide a helpful

introduction to Section 1 of this part of the module. You may find it helpful to take notes as you listen.

Listen:
Apostolic Conversations 2 – Marks of Apostleship [2]
Tim Jack and Steven Anderson with Alistair Matheson; Glasgow, 2020.

Read Appendix 1: *Apostolic Revelation*, Phelim Doherty, 2016

Read Appendix 2:
Identifying Apostleship, National Leadership Team of the Apostolic Church (UK), 2016

The modern dictionary gives some attempted definitions:

* each of the twelve chief disciples of Jesus Christ;

* an important early Christian teacher or pioneering missionary;

* a vigorous and pioneering advocate or supporter of a particular policy, idea, or cause.

The first two suggest that an apostle belongs in history, in the first century specifically.

The third is taken from modern life and could be used in various spheres of business and political life.

Dr C. Peter Wagner, who wrote a great deal on modern day apostles, briefly defines an 'Apostle' as *"a Christian leader who is gifted, taught, and commissioned by God with the authority to establish the foundational government of the Church within an assigned sphere of ministry by hearing what the Spirit is saying to the churches and by setting things in order accordingly for the advancement of the Kingdom of God."* This is by no means a comprehensive definition.

Che Ann, in his book *Modern-Day Apostles*, states: *"An apostle is a Christ-like ambassador with extraordinary authority, called and sent out by Jesus Christ with a specific assignment to align the Church to bring heaven's culture to earth and to fulfil the mandate to disciple nations."*

David Cannistraci, in *Apostles and the Emerging Apostolic Movement*, writes, *"An apostle ... one who is called and sent by Christ to have the spiritual authority, character, gifts and abilities to successfully reach and establish people in Kingdom truth and order, especially through founding and overseeing local churches."*

What do we learn from the New Testament usage?

The word for apostle in the New Testament Greek means 'one who is sent.' This implies being sent by someone and carrying the authorisation of the sender. God the Father sent His Son into the world, and Jesus in turn sends His disciples out into the world (John 20:21).

Jesus chose twelve particular disciples from those who were following Him, designating them 'apostles' (Luke 6:13), though they were otherwise referred to as 'the disciples' or 'the twelve' until Jesus starts sending them out as His representatives doing what He did (see Matthew 10:2; Mark 6:30; Luke 9:10).

There is another word that could be used to simply mean 'send' but Jesus, and in turn the New Testament writers, specifically use the word 'apostle' as it has a more technical meaning. Indeed Jesus and the New Testament writers use two key words that are taken from their time and from Greek/Roman culture. Those words are 'apostle' and 'ekklesia' which has traditionally been translated as 'church.' (We will examine this fully in Section 4.)

In New Testament times an apostle was someone who carried a particular role in Roman society. As the Roman Empire spread one of their major aims was to establish Roman colonies throughout the world. These would be cities that adopted the culture of Rome so much so that if the Emperor visited he would feel at home. Apostles were those who were sent as ambassadors and representatives of Rome to bring this culture to these places. It was an official role with the backing of the Emperor.

Likewise, New Testament apostles were those who were sent and commissioned by the Lord, with His authority, to go and establish heaven's culture, the culture of the Kingdom of God, wherever they went.

Being an apostolic people is not about some having the title 'Apostle' but about recognising apostolic functions which some will lead in as the people of God go in Jesus' name and authority to establish the culture of His Kingdom, planting and building Christian communities that influence the world around them.

Reflective Question:

6. Considering the above definitions how would you describe an apostle?

CHAPTER 7:

CHRIST OUR APOSTLE

"Therefore, holy brethren, partakers of a heavenly calling, consider Jesus, the Apostle and High Priest of our confession; He was faithful to Him who appointed Him." Hebrews 3:1-2a

Jesus was the first Apostle of the New Covenant. John the Baptist came as a prophet preparing the way for the One who was to come, the One sent out from the Father. As the first and primary Apostle, Jesus calls and sends others, and He sets the standard in every way. So Hebrews 3:1 tells us to 'consider' Jesus; fixing our eyes and minds upon Him, observing, perceiving and understanding Him.

Jesus is the prime example of apostolic ministry

Jesus was sent by the Father. He knew who He was. He understood where he had come from, that He had come with a purpose and He knew what that was. *"The Son of Man did not come to be served, but to serve, and to give His life a ransom for many"* (Matthew 20:28); *"For the Son of Man has come to seek and save that which was lost."* (Luke 19:10)

Jesus did not come for His own benefit, but to serve and give of Himself in the ultimate way. He came to seek and to save lost people and even more than that. He came to restore *'that which was lost.'* What was lost? The role and authority of humankind on the earth that God gave in the Garden was lost to Satan. Jesus came to take that authority back and then give those keys back to His apostles and to His people, the church. He came to redeem us through the cross, and also to restore our God ordained function to bring the life-giving rule of God on earth. *'Your Kingdom come, Your will be done, on earth as it is in heaven!'*

Jesus reveals the character required for apostolic ministry

Jesus overcame all the temptations of the evil one, refusing to compromise or give in on any point. He shows the character and integrity of heart that is needed to walk well in the delegated authority that He now imparts to us. We need to appreciate and appropriate the true character of Jesus, not what is always assumed. He wasn't nice or just kind and soft with everyone. He rebuked those living in religious pride, threw money changers out the Temple, but showed deep compassion for those who were harassed and helpless. He exercised the authority of heaven over demons and disease. Maybe a good Scripture to look at is Philippians 2:5-11 ...

> *5 Have this attitude in yourselves which was also in Christ Jesus, 6 who, although He existed in the form of God, did not regard equality with God a*

thing to be grasped, 7 but emptied Himself, taking the form of a bond-servant, and being made in the likeness of men. 8 Being found in appearance as a man, He humbled Himself by becoming obedient to the point of death, even death on a cross. 9 For this reason also, God highly exalted Him, and bestowed on Him the name which is above every name, 10 so that at the name of Jesus every knee will bow, of those who are in heaven and on earth and under the earth, 11 and that every tongue will confess that Jesus Christ is Lord, to the glory of God the Father.

Jesus did not exalt Himself, in fact quite the opposite; therefore, God highly exalts Him at the right time. He didn't grasp at any exaltation, but emptied and humbled Himself as a bondservant or slave, being fully obedient to the will of the One who sent Him.

Apostolic ministry must be in that attitude and heart that exalts Jesus not us, characterised by humility and obedience.

Reflective Question:

7. What are the key attributes that Jesus models for us in leadership roles?

CHAPTER 8:

ASCENSION GIFT MINISTRIES – OVERVIEW AND PURPOSE

Why call them 'ascension gifts'?

As Jesus ascended into the heavens He gave these gift ministries to His people, His church (Ephesians 4:7-12). Jesus had been the representative apostle, prophet, evangelist, pastor (shepherd) and teacher. He would no longer operate on the earth in that way, in the incarnate flesh, but will release His gifts into and through His people. He specifically calls and enables certain people to function in these aspects of His ministry.

What is each of these?

We have already given definition to the ministry of *apostle*, and will go on to develop that further.

The prophet in the New Covenant may have similarities to those in the Old Covenant but is also quite different. No longer is the prophet the one who sees and hears from God for the people. All born again believers can see and hear from the Spirit of God. The prophet is one who grows sufficiently in this ministry to operate in a mature and seasoned way, and therefore can train and equip others to operate in prophetic gifting.

The evangelist is the messenger who brings good news, both announcing and demonstrating the good news of the Kingdom of God. The evangelist will have an anointing that sees people regularly responding in faith in Jesus Christ, but also operates within the Body of Christ to equip others to have a confidence and ability to testify to the Risen Lord with increasing effectiveness.

The pastor, which is the most overused of these terms in the modern church, does care for the flock of God but is not meant to do this as a solo act. Indeed this oversight is the task of the Elders (see Acts 20:17-32), which is always in the plural and not the work of one person. The pastor, like the other ministry gifts, is to equip the rest of the church to pastor and care for one another.

The teacher is also familiar to the modern church as one who brings insight into the Word of God. Teaching can be communicated in many ways and not just 'from a pulpit.' Often it is most effective with small groups even as Jesus focussed on His twelve disciples and especially the inner three of Peter, James and John. Again, the teacher must equip others to be able to read and study the Word for themselves, to feed themselves, and in turn feed other new believers.

The apostle can and will function in all of the above too, but very importantly brings out the best in each of the others.

Based on Christ's given grace and measure - (Ephesians 4:7)

'To each one grace is given' – the gifts are that, 'gifts.' They are not based on merit and give no means for boasting. Christ gives and gives various measures to various people. Why He gives a greater measure to one and not another we do not always understand but He knows. However, we can grow in grace and see the measure increase as we use it well.

What is their purpose?

Ephesians 4:12-13; *'For the equipping of the saints for the work of service, to the building up of the body of Christ.'* To equip God's people, not to do all the work for them. The Greek word used for 'equip' is *katartismos* a term with wide ranging meaning. It was used of the disciples mending their nets (Mark 1:19) and has the following meanings: to repair, to make fit for purpose; to restore, to realign (it was used of surgeons realigning broken bones); to furnish, to make complete. There are both training and healing aspects to this word.

This 'equipping' has the dual purposes of enabling God's people to function effectively and fruitfully in works of service, and in that process to be built up in the Lord and in their faith.

Are these purposes fulfilled yet?

This equipping and building up is to be 'until we all attain to the unity of the faith, and of the knowledge of the Son of God, to a mature man, to the measure of the stature which belongs to the fullness of Christ.' A complicated sentence but the clear conclusion would be that we as the body of Christ are still moving in that direction and have not yet got there! Therefore the ministries of apostles, prophets, evangelists, pastors and teachers are still very much needed to be operating today.

How do they converge and work together?

It is important that we have the five ascension gift ministries functioning well today. It is also crucial that they operate together, in a unison that brings the best out of each one. We have at times witnessed local church situations benefit from one or two of these gifts at one time, and then shift emphasis when new leadership comes in which operates in different gifts. The need is to have the whole complement functioning together and in godly order.

Something of the order or priority is revealed in 1 Corinthians 12:28 where Paul says that God appointed first apostles, second prophets, third teachers, then miracles, gifts of healing and so on.

First we note that this is a slightly different list from Ephesians 4 – no mention of evangelists or pastors, but miracles and healing. Second there is an order – a priority of function. That is not to say that one person is more important or special – Paul's teaching about the body in that chapter states otherwise – but that for the body to grow well there is a need for the gift ministries to operate in a priority of process.

The apostle is ultimately the one who holds the others in check and keeps them all functioning towards the same purpose – building the church to fulfill the Great Commission. The apostle sees the value of what each of the other gifts brings, and brings a convergence that brings the best of each together in the most effective manner.

How might they operate today?

Will each local church have all five ministry gifts operating at a mature level? That is not likely but apostles and prophets especially will operate within spheres (2 Corinthians 10:13, 15). So within a region or a particular stream of church life apostles and prophets may function locally and trans-locally in their purposes. Evangelists, pastors and teachers may do likewise being both local and trans-local. It is primarily Elders (Overseers) who only function in their local situation.

Reflective Question:

8. What is the difference between a hierarchy of ministries and a priority of function of those ministries?

CHAPTER 9:

WHAT DO WE MEAN BY 'CHURCH'?

Let's recap on some of the key thoughts from Section 1.

* What do we mean by 'the church'?
* Why is the church important?
* How does the church function?
* What are we good at, and what are we lacking?

New Testament pictures of the church:

Remember the great biblical metaphors for church:

* Body of Christ – Ephesians 1:22-23; Col. 2:19
* Family (Household) of God – Ephesians 2:18-19
* Temple – Ephesians 2:20-21; I Corinthians 3:16-17
* Bride of Christ – Ephesians 5:25-27
* Army of God – Ephesians 6:10-13; II Corinthians 10:3-5

Meaning of ekklesia

Matthew 16:13-19 and 18:15-20

The word 'church' is both a wrong and unhelpful translation of the Greek NT term 'ekklesia.' It comes from quite a different root and has led to much misunderstanding.

The *ekklesia* was 'a group of citizens called out for governmental purposes.' This included military strategy and election of magistrates. They could also be a small group who listened to and recorded what the king/emperor said and acted to see his will implemented.

The parallels seem clear – we are citizens of heaven living on earth, called together under Christ for the purpose of implementing His will/kingdom on earth as in heaven. We of course do this in a quite different manner.

This is what Jesus is talking about in the only two times that He uses the term – Matthew 16:13-19 and 18:15-20. Much more can be gone into in these passages but a main point is that on both occasions Jesus refers to 'binding and loosing' suggesting this is a primary purpose of His *ekklesia*.

So what does that look like for us? What are we binding and what are we loosing? Essentially we bind what God binds and loose what He looses, and loose what Satan binds and bind what Satan looses (e.g. Luke 13:16, John 11:44).

This activity of binding and loosing opens the way for much greater effectiveness for the Good News of the Kingdom to spread.

If this is what Jesus had in mind when He said He would build His 'church' then what adjustments do we need to make to how we live this out as 21st century communities of faith?

If apostolic ministry is to be restored and effective then in what ways is this *ekklesia* an apostolic community? What are to be our key practices? What are we to value? What is our culture to be like?

The church is a *community* or family with apostolic fathers and mothers.

* *His community* – we value Christ's Presence among us. He is present.

* *House of worship and prayer* – in response to His Presence we worship. In response to His voice and revelation through the Spirit we pray, binding and loosing, calling forth the Kingdom of God upon the earth.

* *Equipping base* where God's people are restored, healed, aligned, trained and taught so as to be made fit and ready to engage in mission to the society around us.

* *A community of signs, wonders and miracles* that demonstrate the power of God, opening doors for and confirming the Good News of the Kingdom.

* *A community marked by great generosity* – we live to give. Freely we have received and freely we give.

* *A mission base*, sending out and releasing each one

to be an effective witness to Christ, making disciples who will become part of this community.

Reflective Question:

9. If you were leading a local church, what would you consider the most important features to build into it?

CHAPTER 10:

CHURCH MODELS IN ACTS – JERUSALEM, ANTIOCH AND EPHESUS

Not all the churches in the New Testament were alike. Even in the earliest days of the Book of Acts we can see different models of church with different emphasis.

There appears to be a progression throughout Acts which we can trace primarily through the models of church in Jerusalem, Antioch and Ephesus.

The Jerusalem church set the tone and had many great attributes as God moved among them and they saw great increase – Acts 2:41-47. However, they did not appear to actively engage in the full extent of Jesus' command to be His witnesses also in Judea, Samaria and to the ends of the earth (Acts 1:8). It took persecution to scatter them and begin the spread outside of Jerusalem (Acts 8:4ff). Neither did they seem to be prepared to cross the divide into the Gentiles. This wouldn't start to happen until the great shift that takes place with Peter's vision and Cornelius' household in Acts 10.

After the first Gentiles come to faith there was still resistance and difficulty with this idea. However, some believers from Cyprus and Cyrene started speaking to Greeks (Acts 11:20-21) seeing great responsiveness. This was the start of the church in Antioch. True to its foundations this church would become a missionary sending centre (Acts 13:1-3) and the home base for Paul. Going from and returning to Antioch, Paul and his companions planted several churches in other cities.

Features of the Antioch church:

1. Established through breaking new ground - 11:19-20

2. Celebrated what God was doing - 11:20

3. Consolidatind teaching - 11:26

4. Responded to prophetic words - 11:27-30

5. Extreme generosity in attitude to finance and people - 11:29; 13:3

6. Worsipped and fasted, ministering to the Lord - 13:2

7. Listening to the Holy Spirit - 13:2

Paul stayed for various lengths of time in different places: some very short, often due to persecution; others longer like Corinth for 18 months, and then Ephesus for around three years.

It is *Ephesus* that becomes a new base for Paul – a base for equipping and sending out many to spread the good news and to plant churches. The whole region heard the word of the Lord (Acts 19:10) while Paul remained in Ephesus. Ephesus was a city with a major demonic stronghold yet Paul brings great breakthrough by means of extraordinary miracles (19:11) and exposing the occult practices.

At **Ephesus** (Acts 19) Paul's apostolic ministry led to:

* Believers being filled with the Holy Spirit, speaking in tongues and prophesying (v. 6);

* People being equipped to share the good news and plant churches (vv. 9-10);

* The breaking of the demonic stronghold over the city (vv. 18-20; v. 23ff.).

Reflective Question:

10. Read the relevant chapters of Acts: Jerusalem (2-6); Antioch (11:19-30; 13:1-3; 14:26-28); and Ephesus (19-20).

What do you notice about each church in each city, and what can we learn from these different situations and models?

CHAPTER 11:

FOUNDATION OF APOSTLES AND PROPHETS

> "... God's household, having been built on the foundation of the apostles and prophets, Christ Jesus Himself being the cornerstone."
> Ephesians 2:19-20

It is apostolic and prophetic ministry that lays the foundations for the building of the church, God's household, the *ekklesia*. Other most valid ministries are necessary, but to be most effective they need to build on the best foundation, and all be aligned to Jesus Christ as the cornerstone of the whole building.

What does 'the foundation of the apostles and prophets' mean? What does this look like and what might it look like today?

If the earliest churches were built on this foundation so should every church planted since. We are built with Christ as the cornerstone, the ultimate foundation (1 Corinthians 3:11). Then we are built on the apostolic teaching of the New Testament. But who are the prophets? The Old Testament ones or unnamed New Testament prophets? While we build on Christ and the Word, do we not also need to have these very foundations laid by apostolic ministry that builds as a wise master builder (1 Corinthians 3:10)? Do we not benefit from prophetic ministry that brings encouragement and revelation from the Spirit about where, when and how to build?

The church is built on revelation and authority (Matthew 16:13-19). Jesus builds His church on this rock of revelation – a true understanding of who He is. Alongside this, Jesus gives the keys of the Kingdom which represent authority. It is the apostles and prophets who lead the way in bringing a fuller revelation and a true understanding of the authority we are given and the knowledge of how to operate in that authority.

The following article will hopefully develop your understanding of prophetic gifting and the ministry of prophet in the church today.

Read Appendix 3: *New Testament Prophecy and Prophets*, Alistair Matheson, 2020

Reflective Question:

11. What makes apostles and prophets necessary to the establishing of maturing and fruitful churches?

CHAPTER 12:

APOSTOLIC HISTORY – WHY WAS APOSTOLIC MINISTRY MARGINALISED?

If apostolic ministry seemed so important and prevalent in New Testament times, why did it become so marginalised in later centuries?

False Apostles

Even in the earliest times of the New Testament we find the appearance of false apostles. Paul has to contend with some who operated out of wrong motives (2 Corinthians 11:13), and the Lord warns the church in Ephesus of such apostles in Revelation 2:2. The New Testament also warns of false prophets (Matthew 7:15; 24:11; 1 John 4:1), false teaching and teachers (1 Timothy 1:3; 2 Peter 2:1), and even false believers (2 Corinthians 11:36; Galatians 2:4). The appearance of the false gives warning to be discerning but also suggests that the real exists! Sometimes a reaction based in fear has been to dismiss all in case of the deception of the false.

Papal succession

The Roman Catholic Church has taught that the Pope is part of an apostolic succession going back to Peter as the first one. Along with this is the doctrine of papal infallibility in matters of teaching truth. Martin Luther, along with other Reformers, rejected both of these teachings. These Reformers along with this tended to also promote cessationism, the belief that miracles, spirituals gifts, apostles and prophets all ceased at the end of the 1st century.

Dismissal of spiritual gifts and miracles to the first century

The cessationist viewpoint appeared long before the Reformers. Pope Gregory the Great, who was Pope from 590 to 604 AD, wrote that *"the sick are to be admonished that they feel themselves to be sons of God in that the scourge of discipline chastises them."* (Book of Pastoral Rule). Sickness began to be viewed as identifying with the sufferings of Jesus, and therefore a discipline resulting in blessing. We see this influence throughout much of the church today still.

Christendom

In 324 AD the Roman emperor Constantine proclaimed that Christianity was to be the official religion of the Roman Empire. While this put a stop to the persecution of believers, it also had the effect of diluting the church and bringing in a mixture of the old pagan practices. Christianity became a politically organised, religious church lacking God's power and life.

Over-emphasis on the pastoral and parish models

Out of Christendom grew an over-emphasis on models of church designed to keep the faithful rather than reach the lost. Teachers were needed to instruct the people and pastors to look after the flock. Apostles, prophets and evangelists appeared redundant.

Reflective Question:

12. While learning from the past, what should we be aware of when looking to recognise and release apostles today?

CHAPTER 13:

CHARACTERISTICS AND FUNCTIONS OF AN APOSTOLIC MINISTRY

The following is not an exhaustive list, but these are certainly among the prominent features of an apostolic ministry.

Characteristics

- **Called, Commissioned and Sent** – Romans 1:1; 1 Corinthians 1:1; Acts 13:2-3

Apostles are not selected by men and women but called by God. The church recognises such calling and under the direction of the Holy Spirit commissions and releases these apostles to function in their calling.

- **Christlikeness** – Romans 8:29; 1 Corinthians 4:16

All believers are called and destined to be conformed to the likeness of Jesus Christ. If apostles are to set an example to be imitated then how important it is that they are walking in a growing Christlikeness. As they represent Christ the Apostle so His life and nature must be recognisable in them.

- **Authority** – 2 Corinthians 10:8; 13:10

This authority Paul speaks of is clearly for building up, not tearing down. It is for the equipping, strengthening and releasing of the Body of Christ. Such authority is life giving. Authority can of course be misused to control, dominate and manipulate and this must be confronted and resisted. To exercise true authority the apostle must be under the Lord's authority and accountable to other leaders in the church.

- **Alignment** – 1 Corinthians 12:28

It is important that apostles are properly aligned with prophets, teachers and other gift ministries, and rightly aligned with other apostles who will enhance one another's ministries.

- **Spheres** – 2 Corinthians 10:15-16

The Scripture suggests that different apostles were assigned certain spheres by the call of God and by the Holy Spirit. This may be geographical or ethnic or some other sphere of life.

- **Breakthrough and build**

The Book of Acts relates many breakthroughs of the apostles Peter, Paul and others and of their apostolic teams. But such breakthroughs need to be built upon for lasting impact. In 1 Corinthians 3:10 Paul describes himself as 'a wise master builder' – apostles build solid foundations and others may build upon these.

- **Accessing resources (gathering)** – Acts 4:35-37

People laid their gifts at the apostles' feet for them to distribute wisely and according to the need. Some, like Barnabas, brought significant gifts. Apostles gather resources – of people, of finance and more.

- **Work with prophets** – Ephesians 2:20; Acts 16:25-26 (15:22-32)

Paul, an apostle, and Silas, a prophet, teamed up and brought great breakthrough in Philippi. The apostle-prophet combination is very effective in the work of God.

- **Finishing well** – Acts 20:24; 2 Timothy 4:7; Philippians 3:12-14

Apostles must complete the tasks given to them. As master builders they must finish the work. Sometimes that finishing is to hand on to someone else so the ministry continues well after the have moved on.

Functions

- **Casting vision**

Paul says that he 'was not disobedient to the heavenly vision' (Acts 26:19). Paul received vision and also cast it to others in the churches he planted and in those who came alongside him in the work.

- **Breaking through and building**

At times to teach at length (Acts 2:42; 11:26; 19:10). This included spiritual warfare – binding and loosing, high praises, prayer, the Word, signs and wonders – that broke hindering and ruling spirits (c.f. Acts 19:11-20)

- **Governing and appointing elders**

Acts 14:23; *"When they had appointed elders for them in every church, having prayed with fasting, they commended them to the Lord in whom they had believed."*

- **Testifying with power: miracles, signs and wonders**

2 Corinthians 12:12; *"The signs of a true apostle were performed among you with all perseverance, by signs and wonders and miracles."* (See also,

Acts 4:33; 5:12)

- **Equipping and mobilising believers**

In Ephesus, this appeared to lead to church plants all over the region (Acts 19:10).

- **Imparting spiritual gifts**

Romans 1:11; *"For I long to see you so that I may impart some spiritual gift to you, that you may be established..."*

- **Strengthening and encouraging**

Acts 14:21-22; *"After they had preached the gospel to that city and had made many disciples, they returned to Lystra and to Iconium and to Antioch, strengthening the souls of the disciples, encouraging them to continue in the faith, and saying, 'Through many tribulations we must enter the kingdom of God.'"*

- **Resolving conflict**

This is seen especially in Paul's letters to the Corinthians, Galatians and others.

- **Bringing a convergence of other ministries**

Apostles and their teams carried a significant authority to break new ground and to build up the Body, releasing other ascension gift ministries into ministering with authority in their own callings and spheres.

Reflective Questions:

13.1.1. In what ways do you see that apostolic ministry brings breakthrough and builds, and why is it necessary to build on the breakthrough?

13.1.2. What examples have you observed and experienced of apostolic ministry functioning?

CHAPTER 14:

APOSTOLIC TEAMS

Paul and others formed apostolic teams. From the start, Jesus sent out His disciples in twos for good reasons. Two or more gives the power of agreement (Matthew 18:19), a protection and positive accountability, whereas ministering and especially travelling alone can leave a minister of Christ more vulnerable to attack, accusation and the negative effects of loneliness.

They were based somewhere – for example, Paul in Antioch – and went out from there. It is important that those who travel within the body of Christ have a proper base where they receive covering and have a good sense of accountability to. Paul and his teams would go from Antioch and also return and report back (Acts 14:26-28).

Apostolic teams functioned locally and trans-locally (residential and mobile). Their numbers changed – different ones joined and left, and they seemed to increase in size (Acts 20:4). Another prominent feature is that they functioned with prophets (Ephesians 2:20; Acts 11:27; 15:32, 40) and teachers (Acts 13:1; 1 Corinthians 12:28). Apostles also appointed elders, generally when they moved on (14:23).

There are many different ways that apostolic teams can relate, collaborate and function together in the 21st century, especially with resources of information and communication technology and modern networks of regional and global travel that were unimaginable in the first century. The potential is immeasurable, but what is needed is the vision and desire to develop the spiritual principles and dynamics of team ministry that have been evident since the Book of Acts.

One thing we discover is that apostolic teams were led by an apostle but teams might consist of various ministry gifts.

Explore the following texts (and others that may cross-reference), and take what you discover into the reflective questions below: Acts 11:27; 13:1; 14:23; 15:32, 40; 20:4; I Corinthians 12:28; and Ephesians 2:20.

Reflective Question:

14.1.1. Why is 'team ministry' important?
14.1.2. What are its benefits and challenges?

CHAPTER 15:

BEING AN APOSTOLIC PEOPLE – POSTOLIC CULTURE

Take time to reflect on the following brief article entitled 'Five Apostolic Values' by Tim Jack, former National Leader of the Apostolic Church UK, which unpacks some of the key values that underpin apostolic culture.

Five Apostolic Values

Everything flows to us from God's great love, by His grace. Grace is not a commodity. Grace is God's love coming to us in Jesus Christ.

This grace is rooted in the communion between Jesus and the Father. It comes from the presence of the Triune God. This is where the power for our mission flows from. So, we need to be people of the presence of God. The gracious power of the presence of God melts the power of hostility and indifference.

The Church is the Body of Christ, so it is not separate from Christ.

An apostolic church is not people of theory – it is a people crafted to be carriers of a ministry that displays to the world something of the humility, something of the servant-hood, something of the power of God that comes and is delivered by faith. Apostolic people understand the message of Ephesians chapter 4. They understood that there is a gift to the church from the ascended Christ of the 'fivefold ministry' – not to form a hierarchy, but to be a group of people who equip the saints.

To be genuinely apostolic, the church needs these five Apostolic Values:

1) An Apostolic Church is *Christ-centred*

    Jesus Christ is the centre of everything. Everything is from Him, through Him and to Him. *"Having made known to us the mystery of His will, according to His good pleasure which He purposed in Himself, that in the dispensation of the fullness of the times He might gather together in one all things in Christ, both which are in heaven and which are on earth—in Him."* (Ephesians 1:9-10). This is God's plan, to bring everything together under Jesus Christ.

2) An Apostolic Church is *Theocratic*

    If Christ is the Head of the Church, then He is the One who rules the Church. Jesus *'moves among the candlesticks'* (Revelation 1:12-13) – He is not far away. He is God with us. And He rules His Church through the ministries He raises up of apostles, prophets, evangelists, pastors and teachers.

3) An Apostolic Church is *Covenantal*

We're washed in the same blood, filled with the same Spirit and called to the same mandate. And so we resolve issues properly – we do not run away. Grace enables us to resolve whatever issues we might have, growing up together into Christ the Head.

4) An Apostolic Church is *Pentecostal*

There are young people in Pentecostal churches who have never heard prophecy or seen a healing. An apostolic people is open to the presence of God. Many churches are content with a changed atmosphere, but that is not Pentecost! Manifestations of the Spirit are not enough. On the Day of Pentecost, they broke out of the room and spoke Christ to people.

5) An Apostolic Church is *Missional*

You cannot separate Christ from mission! In Acts 1:8 we are told that the Holy Spirit gives power to witness to Jesus. Under His power the Church will be bold and confident enough to engage society regardless of its hostility. Hostility melts away before true servant-hood and true humility. The Holy Spirit does a whole range of things in Acts, but an apostolic people does not forget that their purpose is to engage in meaningful witness to a broken world.

The following audio file provides a helpful development of these key values that articulate underpin apostolic culture. You may find it helpful to take notes as you listen.

Watch: Apostolic Conversations 3 – Apostolic Values [5] Tim Jack and Steven Anderson with Alistair Matheson; Glasgow, 2020

FINAL ASSIGNMENT

Please ensure that the following assignment is completed and submitted digitally to Baton Administration by the date of your final Supervisor Appointment.

On the basis of your study of Scripture, recommended reading and reflective responses in this module, produce a 2,000–3,000 word paper entitled, 'An Apostolic People for the 21st Century'.

The following bulleted questions needn't be addressed in any particular order, but they should be engaged with in the course of your paper:

　　* What are the prominent features of an apostolic people?

　　* How does the culture of churches in the west-

ern world today measure up with these?

* What marks and features of an apostolic culture would merit special emphasis of attention in your own church context?

* Describe an apostolic people you would love to see.

APPENDIX 1:

Apostolic Revelation

Phelim Doherty, 2016

All that glitters is not gold!

Apostolic revelation on the Church and Christ

I believe the Holy Spirit's strategy to strengthen the Church is timeless and trans-cultural, because it was never based on natural human wisdom, but on raising the vision, the thinking of believers, out of the natural realm and into the heavenly realm, or as the apostle Paul described it in Ephesians 4; to grow up believers into the head, the mind of Christ.

- Bridges have a purpose; to enable people to get to the other side of a natural obstacle. Bridges are not built so that a country can claim to have bridges!

- Apostolic teaching is not about believing in apostles, prophets, evangelists, pastors and teachers. These ascension ministries are called to ascend (raise up) believers to transcend a natural obstacle; their natural earthly thinking and into a new way of thinking and a new way of living, called life 'in Christ'. True ascension ministry produces a manifestation of ascension life (Colossians 3:1-4).

"What no eye has seen, what no ear has heard, and what no human mind has conceive – the things God has prepared for those who love him – these are things that God has revealed to us by His Spirit." (I Corinthians 2:9, 10)

Notice what the Spirit comes to reveal: not what needs to be done, but what has already been prepared.

God already has prepared a heavenly vision for us, and it is nothing less than His heavenly vision *of* us.

It is as His heavenly vision is declared over His people, that they start to rise up to live *from* that vision, for faith comes by hearing.

The greatest blessing is revelation and it is *the* blessing by which Christ builds His Church. This is why it is necessary to pray for revelation across any movement that aspires to be apostolic.

"Blessed are you Simon bar Jonah, for flesh and blood has not revealed this to you, but my Father who is in heaven." (Matthew 16:17)

Jesus declared, *"This is the rock I will build my Church on."* He was speaking of revelation from the Father, of the person and work of Christ (– what the apostle Paul summed up his gospel message as: *"Christ and Him crucified."*).

This is where our understanding of what the gospel is and what it is not, is fundamental. The Church is not built on good advice, but good news!

"As you received Him, so walk in Him" (Colossians 2:6)

You and I received Him by a revelation of His Spirit and so that is how we are to walk through the days ahead: by settling not for flesh and blood, but for nothing less than revelation from above.

We need to pray for every part of the Apostolic fellowship to rise in the revelation of Christ and Him crucified and what that means for us who are *in* Him.

I would like to challenge us to look beyond and pray beyond the Apostolic Church as we now see it, and begin to pray for the Apostolic Church as Christ sees it.

In that famous apostolic scripture from Ephesians 4, is not primarily about the fivefold ministries, it is about growing up into the head, who is Christ.

The ministry gifts are of Him, to raise up a people who would live in Him.

The Apostolic Church is known for believing in ascension ministries.

- but those gifts were not given that men may believe in ascension ministries;
- they were given that men would live in ascension life.

A recent National Women's Report for the Apostolic Church noted the following:

"We have noticed since we started that many women do not know who they are in Christ and the authority they have been given through Jesus."

The growth that God desires to see in His body is not just about physical size, but about maturity. But it's not an either–or choice. We want both.

The Holy Spirit has for us a fresh revelation across this fellowship, of Christ's vision of maturity, His glorious vision of what a mature Church looks like.

We have such a picture of what the mature Christ looks like, manifested in human form.

I would like to use one scripture as an aid to our prayers for revelation, so that we can pray about three revelations of maturity that the Lord would

AN APOSTOLIC PEOPLE

have His body grow in.

John 13

Verse 1: "Jesus knew His hour had come and, having loved His disciples, He loved them to the end."

That's an introduction to something Jesus is about to do; He is about to demonstrate what mature love looks like and what mature love does in the end.

Our picture to pray from is in verses 3–5: "3 Jesus, knowing that the Father had given all things into His hands, and that He had come from God and was going to God, 4 rose from supper and laid aside His garments, took a towel and girded Himself. 5 After that, He poured water into a basin and began to wash the disciples' feet, and to wipe them with the towel with which He was girded."

If we want to pray for the growth of an Apostolic fellowship across the world, then let us pray for a growth sourced and sustained by nothing less than a revelation of Christ and His ascended mature Church; that we may rise up into that vision, His vision of us.

In these verses are three revelations that we must grow in, to grow as the ascended mature body of Christ, to grow up into Christ (Ephesians 4:15).

1.

Verse 3: "Jesus, knowing that the Father had given all things into His hands."

The revelation of the sufficiency of Christ's provision in our lives.

It is time to stop asking for more, when we have yet to recognise the enormity of what He has already given us in Christ.

There are so many areas we could apply this to, but to remain focused, I would like us to think just on the issue of leadership, at every level of our fellowship across the nations: families, assemblies, regions and national councils.

We have prayed often for ascension ministries to be raised up in our land and across the wider mission fields. I would find it hard to believe that the Lord has not already sent the answer. Would He not say to us what He said to the prophet Daniel: "From the first day you prayed, you were heard and the answers despatched".

In Mark 11:24, Jesus speaks of praying from a revelation of what we already have. "Therefore I tell you, whatever you ask for in prayer, believe that you have received it, and it will be yours."

We are not going to pray that God would send more leaders. We are going to pray for revelation across the body of the sufficiency of Christ's provision;

that the leaders, these giftings and callings, have been given.

Let us pray that they would be seen. Let us pray for a revelation that what we have been asking for, we now have and as we look again, we will see what we could not see before.

Elijah kept sending his servant to look again for the promised rain. As we go to our assemblies and our various nations, we want to look again by the Spirit of God and see that His promises are Yes and Amen.

Hannah had cried out for years for fruit in her womb. Through a word from the priest at the temple, revelation came and she saw her child as already given and her countenance changed and she went home and conceived.

Let's pray that many will rise from the place of prayer with a revelation of their union with Christ as 'already given' and conceive great fruit from that revelation.

2.

Verse 3: "Jesus ... knowing that He had come from God and was going to God".

The revelation of our calling and our destiny in the body of Christ; our identity in Christ!

The second revelation we can pray for across the Apostolic Church, is that of our identity in Christ, that we may take our place to function in His body.

(So many of us for so many years, in not knowing who we are – sons of the living God – have fallen prey to legalism, attempting to earn what is already ours, the blessing of God.)

We are not an orphan church. We have a generous Father who has withheld in Christ no good thing from us (Romans 8:32): "We have been blessed in the heavenly realms with every blessing in Christ." (Ephesians 1:3)

Again, in this area let us not be a Church praying for God to release what has already been released to us: His blessing and favour. Rather, let us see by the Spirit, where His blessing now is: in Christ.

We have no calling to ask God to bless our lives or our work.

You don't have a life. You died and so did I.

The Cross is an I with a stroke through it.

Galatians 2: "20 I have been crucified with Christ; it is no longer I who live, but Christ lives in me; and the life which I now live in the flesh I live by faith in the Son of God, who loved me and gave Himself for me. 21 I do not set aside the grace of God; for if righteousness comes through the law, then Christ died in vain."

The grace of God is abundant for all in Christ, but if we, in our confusion over our identity, start to try and earn the approval of God, through our performance, we estrange ourselves from the grace of God. (See Galatians 5:4)

The apostolic fellowship is not the identity that we should draw life from; our historic achievements or traditions, glorious though they may appear to us, are only glitter compared to the gold of our identity in Christ.

It is by His name and His Spirit that we live and move and have our being. Spirit graced humility is not thinking less of ourselves, but thinking of our 'selves' less. A growing revelation of our union with Christ brings a growing revelation of union with His body, the wider Church.

Let us pray for a revelation of where we came from and where we are going; that Christ is our life from start to finish, the author and the finisher.

It's is not our job to finish what He started.

He will complete the good work He began in us. Let us allow His Holy Spirit to so convince us of this, that we effectively live as if it is already done; for that is where heaven lives; in the light of the finished work. This is what it is to 'work out your salvation', to live from His finished work, to live from whom His Spirit declares us to be: complete in Him.

Let's pray for every area of the worldwide fellowship to grow in this revelation of their true identity in Christ.

We died together with Him, we were buried together with Him, we rose together with Him and we are seated together with Him in Christ in the heavenly realms. Let us so set our minds on these heavenly truths that our thinking, and so our living, ascends into righteousness, peace and joy (Romans 14:17), which will be the manifestation of the Kingdom on the earth, as it is in heaven!

3.

Verses 4–5: "4 Jesus rose from supper and laid aside His garments, took a towel and girded Himself. 5 After that, He poured water into a basin and began to wash the disciples' feet, and to wipe them with the towel with which He was girded."

Revelation of our call as a movement: to serve the body of Christ.

Here we see the fruit of revelation: character. And here we see that the character of the mature Christ and the characteristic of every mature believer or movement of believers, is a life poured out for others.

Any life that has found its source in the eternal God, knows now that it cannot lose anything by pouring itself out!

The revelation of Christ as our life sets us free from ourselves and all the limits of the natural man, all the limits of living as mere natural men and women, especially the limit that self-consciousness puts on our ability to pour out our lives.

If as individuals and as an Apostolic movement, we never grow beyond thinking of self-preservation, then we will never fulfil our destiny of maturity: to give ourselves away for the rest of the body.

In this final part of our picture of maturity, Christ sets aside His garments (glory) to bind to Himself the garment of a servant.

- I will know that I have matured when I no longer hear myself thinking before every action, "What will this do for me?"

- We will know the Apostolic Fellowship is rising, is blossoming into a greater maturity, when we no longer hear ourselves talk of our movement, as if we were raised up to be something apart from the rest of the body of Christ!

The mature Church lives to serve and especially serve the household of God.

The great Apostolic truths we read in Ephesians are not speaking of one part of the body maturing, but of the whole body growing and building itself up in love as each part does its work.

We would say to an individual new believer, "If you really want to grow into your destiny, it's all very well enjoying great revelations from the head, but you will discover that you cannot grow beyond a certain point, if you will not connect with the rest of the body, for your ultimate destiny was never to live as an 'I', but to live as an 'us'."

Jesus never taught His disciples to pray, "My Father, give me my daily bread," but "Our Father, give us our daily bread."

That is how we must pray as a movement, with a revelation that 'us' is not just this movement, but the worldwide body of Christ.

So, let us rise up in this revelation of our call: to serve the wider body of Christ and let us begin to pray for them, as we have prayed for revelation for ourselves. Let us pray not just for the 'Apostolic Church' but, in the words of that most ancient of confessions, let us pray for the 'holy catholic and apostolic church', the body of Christ.

Knowing that we are beloved sons, in the security of our identity in Christ, let us set aside our own garments and bind to ourselves the garment of a servant and be a movement that ministers apostolically and prophetically and in every other calling we have been gifted in, into the body of Christ worldwide, that the whole body would mature and prosper, not just the part we know as the 'Apostolic Church'. This is what it means to be truly apostolic, to be 'a movement and not a monument'.

Let us pray for other churches and groups.

If we cannot pray for the other churches in our towns and cities (that in the natural we have viewed as competition), then we are ministering ourselves not Christ, for He laid down His life for them and His Spirit is pouring into them.

APPENDIX 2:

Notes on Identifying Apostleship

National Leadership Team of The Apostolic Church (UK), 2016

Apostle, Greek *apostolos* [apo-, from + stello, I send]; a sent one, one sent forth.

Marks of Apostleship include: authority, testimony, recognition, distinctives and impact.

1. *Authority*

The apostle is sent 'from' and is sent 'to'. There is Authority in both aspects!

Carries "from" as an ambassador/representative; in its nurture it carries authority.

Carries "To" with a message/ministry; in its nature

AN APOSTOLIC PEOPLE

it carries authority.

Authority exists because of who sent it, but also because of who carries it.

Apostolic authority stems from the resurrection of Jesus.

It is Jesus (alive and well) who commissions for service.

Ascension Gifts (Eph 4 vs 11-13) Tokens of triumph and a celebration of victory!

2. *Testimony*

Early Church apostles were some of those who had witnessed the resurrected Jesus. (See Acts 1:21-22)

For Paul, it became an important qualification for him as part of his testimony. (See I Corinthians 9:1)

The encounter was important! They were witnesses of a powerful experience in their life.

In any form of ministry the first point of credibility is around your own testimony, but particularly for the apostle. It starts with the personal encounter with the risen Lord, and you know without a shadow of a doubt that you have been in His presence, that He is alive!

Depending on how you read the text, there are

18-23 named apostles in the New Testament.

Jesus is first, the greatest Apostle.

Jesus' 12 disciples: Peter, James, John, Andrew, Philip, Bartholemew, Thomas, Matthew, James, Thaddeus, Simon, Judas. (Matthias is added later.)

Barnabas and Paul, Epaphroditus, Silas and Timothy, James (brother of Christ), Titus, Apollos,

Andronicus and Junias (Romans 16:7; possibly a woman? ... "Outstanding among the Apostles).

3. *Recognition*

The call of God establishes Apostleship. See Romans 1:1, I Corinthians 1:1, II Corinthians 1:1, I Timothy 1:1, Galatians 1:1.

However, recognition comes from other Apostles.

This is the unique stewardship of God's grace. Apostles will have "grace eyes" and a "grace heart".

They can see the activity of God when no one else can see it. They will believe in someone before any other person can.

Apostleship recognises apostleship, sometimes only the tender shoots of developing growth.

Able to greenhouse, to nurture and protect, to bring to fullness and stature.

We live in the dispensation of grace and this is the administration of grace in the 'house of grace'.

The apostle is the custodian, the house manager while the owner is away.

To have care of all the churches. (See II Corinthians 11:28)

4. *Distinctives*

Architect and Builder. In I Corinthians 3:10, sees the big picture, not just one room or one corner.

Recognises the difference between surface/superficial and foundational problems and is well qualified and called to deal with the foundational.

Pioneering and establishing. Primacy of function, often first on the site.

Revelatory and visionary.

Planting and developing.

Manifesting relevance.

Signs and wonders evident. II Corinthians 12:12 says something about power!

Fathering and mentoring.

Keeping the Faith – a trustee, steward of truth, defender of the faith (See Acts 2:42).

Valuing what is good in the old while stretching out into the new and progressive.

Creating new communities of faith.

Problem solving – includes 'trouble shooting', organising and strategizing.

5. *Impact*

Transmitting, not just reiterating.

Minister of the Spirit: listening and leading towards encounter.

Able to face crisis with confidence, to deal with conflict as an inevitable feature of community, and resolve by finding roots.

Additional notes...

Apostles:
- Understand growth
- Celebrate creativity
- Encourage maturity
- Possess tenacity
- Release anointing
- Reject mediocrity

Characteristics:

- Patience
- Integrity
- Fearlessness
- Wisdom
- Perseverance
- Faith
- Accountability
- Entrepreneurial – business/management?

Important Emphases

- The organisation of the church is not merely a human arrangement.
- We do not believe in anonymous apostleship. (See I Corinthians 9:1-2)
- Apostleship carries burden for The Church. (See I Corinthians 11:28)
- "First of all, apostles." (I Corinthians 12:28)
- Foundational gifts that are indispensable.
- Leadership Role: the apostle who has been "sent from" will know how to "lead to".
- Apostles carry authority with instruction from Jesus. (See II Peter 3:2)
- Apostles have varying degrees of giftedness.

- Ephesians 4:11-13; there is a work of perfecting going on ... "... until we all reach."
- Ascension gifts are relevant and necessary to attain the end goal.
- Expression of the gifts is essential to the peace and unity of the church.
- Absence opens door for confusion, anarchy and ill-discipline.
- Authority administered by gifting and anointing.

"First Apostles" (I Corinthians 12:28):

- Throughout the New Testament, apostles have prominence as significant leaders.
- The nature and power of apostleship in church government remain vital to the church.
- How this works out in practice today is crucial to the life and vitality of The Church.

Aspects to Avoid

- Legalism: Scripture is descriptive not always prescriptive. We cannot easily prescribe and expect to receive. It is a matter of the Spirit not of the law.
- Control: Submission and authority walk hand in hand. Apostleship requires recognition and submission. It should be assertive, never forceful.
- Calls of convenience: Avoid filling vacancies in

structure just to support the structure. It demeans the office and the call.

- Imposition: Apostleship is best received by invitation, not delivered by imposition. It travels smoothly on the relational bridges that are built. A bumpy ride may suggest the wrong route has been used.

- Unrealistic expectation: The Apostle Paul should not be our bench mark.

- Overload of administration: It is a matter of balance. Apostleship can bring life to administration, but equally administration can bring death to Apostleship. Some administration may be required, too much will suffocate.

- Rigidity of structure: The maxim "form follows function" should apply. Apostleship seeks to release, not to restrain. The word used to describe the "sending away" of Paul and Barnabas in Acts 13 is 'apoluo', which has sense of releasing, setting loose and sending away. The stronger word 'apostello' is not used. 'Apoluo' portrays the image of an impatient horse being released from a stable, which gallops away when the door is opened. Church leaders recognise God's calling and remove constraints.

APPENDIX 3:

New Testament Prophecy and Prophets

Alistair Matheson, 2020

"Would that all the Lord's people were prophets, that the Lord would put His Spirit upon them!" (Numbers 11:29)

This was the exclamation of an apparently exasperated Moses to his disciple, Joshua.

Clearly all Moses wanted was to see the message of God 'getting out there'. He didn't really care who the messenger was. All he really cared about was God Himself and the people with whom God was concerned. This has always been the way with God's 'go-betweens' – we ourselves don't really come into it. The heart of the prophet is to serve and honour God by getting His word to those who need it.

Getting back to Moses' cry before Joshua – of course, in the real world, there is little chance that all God's people will be prophets. But has that ever remotely been a danger?!

Shift to the New Testament.

"Earnestly desire spiritual gifts, but especially that you may prophesy!" (I Corinthians 14:1) Paul exhorted the believers in Corinth. *"... For you can all prophesy in turn,"* (I Corinthians 14:31) he went on to allow.

We're in the New Covenant now and for 'prophet' we can read 'church' – or, more accurately, Christ revealing Himself through His whole body, the church. The great subtext to the outpouring of the Holy Spirit at Pentecost statement was not the wonderful things that were actually being declared in the languages of the gathering audience, but the fact that the prophetic word was not being declared by the mouth of a silver-bearded individual, but through the entire assortment of those gathered ... old and young, free and bonded, men and women! (See Acts 2:17-18) This is what had been foretold by an Old Testament prophet, Joel, who could only wistfully look on.

And yet, in the midst of this great collective – the church, which amounts to the equivalent of the Old Testament prophet – we also find a completely new model of prophet, the New Testament prophet, one who is actually equipped to do what Moses had longed for: the equipping of all God's people to become the great God's mouthpiece through whom – to God speaking to Moses this time – *"...all the earth will be filled with the glory of the Lord."* (Numbers 14:21)

The days of the lonesome, 'outsider' prophet of the Old Testament are over. The New Testament prophet, according to Ephesians chapter 4, is one who engages with God's people, sharing his gift with people who have dwelling within them the same Holy Spirit as he does, inspiring, equipping and mobilising them to become a people who collectively express the ministry of The Prophet, Jesus Christ, to all creation. As with the Old Testament prophet, so with a maturing New Testament church: it's not really about individuals, but God Himself, us building each other up in Him, and the world for which Christ died and we have been raised up.

Within that context, the New Testament prophet has also been raised up and as a leadership gift to the church and, according to Ephesians 2:20, alongside the apostle in particular, a foundational and directional ministry through which Christ builds His church (– more on that later).

Before we look at the nature of the prophetic in the church, another very important thing must be said about the difference between the classic Old Testament prophet and the prophetic ministry of the New, relating to the crucial matters of authority and inspiration.

The Old Testament prophets of scripture spoke with an infallibility that came straight from God. Their message was rightly to be accepted and obeyed without question. They did not have, as the church does, a scriptural canon on which to base their authority, and their audience were to assume that they spoke entirely and precisely as God had spoken to them.

Be wary of New Testament 'prophets' who do not recognise personal fallibility and base their authority exclusively on personal 'revelation' (– not that the Spirit doesn't speak supernaturally), no matter how vividly or convincingly such an 'epiphany moment' is described, rather than allow their message to be subject to the authority of Scripture and make their ministry accountable to the God-ordained checks and balances of local church oversight.

Peter makes clear that infallibility is to be found in the *"prophecy of Scripture"* (II Peter 1:19-21), with the prophetic declarations of the Bible to be considered fully authoritative, in the same way as, for example, the words of the prophet Moses were to the children of Israel.

Not so, the New Testament gift of prophecy. Whereas Peter teaches that the church is to be governed by the light of Bible prophecy, Paul teaches the Corinthians very clearly that the New Testament gift of prophecy is to be governed by the church: *"Let two or three prophets speak, and let the others pass judgment."* (I Corinthians 14:29)

As Paul had pointed out in the previous chapter, *"... we know in part and we prophesy in part; ... we see in a mirror dimly ..."* (I Corinthians 13:9, 12) – this clearly couldn't be said of the prophet Moses as he delivered the plans of God, with full authority and in precise detail, *"according to the pattern shown ... on the mount."* (Exodus 25:40)

It's simple: the prophecy of Scripture is infallible and judges us, but the gift of prophecy is fallible and to be judged by us (in light of Scripture and the collective wisdom of church oversight).

If this fundamental truth had been effectively laid, fully understood and clearly communicated through the history of the modern-day Pentecostal and charismatic movements, an huge amount of damage could have been prevented ... and an awful lot of cessationists (those who believe that the charismatic gifts ended with the early church) might have been nicer to those of us who believe that there has never been a Retro-Pentecost Day (that is, a moment when the charismatic gifts were sucked back up to Heaven)!

The New Testament prophet to the church, unlike the Old Testament prophet to Israel, appears to bring confirmation and timing to things already received by the Holy Spirit, in a dispensation where the congregation and all individuals within it experience the indwelling of the Spirit in a way only dreamt of by the prophets of the Old.

Consider, for example, how the prophets appear to operated in Antioch in Acts chapter 13:1-4 ...

> *"Now there were at Antioch, in the church that was there, prophets and teachers: Barnabas, and Simeon who was called Niger, and Lucius of Cyrene, and Manaen who had been brought up with Herod the tetrarch, and Saul. While they were ministering to the Lord and fasting, the Holy Spirit said, "Set apart for Me Barnabas and Saul for the work to which I have called them." Then, when they had fasted and prayed and laid their hands on them, they sent them away. So, being sent out by the Holy Spirit, they went down to Seleucia and from there they sailed to Cyprus."*

Note how the Spirit spoke through the Antioch

prophets, releasing Barnabas and Saul to something which He had already called them. With regard to Paul, for example, we need only back up to Acts chapter 9 to see that this is a conversation that had begun between the Lord and Saul a number of years before, and there was now a confluence of the prophets, Saul, the Antioch team and, most crucially, the Holy Spirit, to release Paul into his full blown apostolic ministry. The same Spirit who had told Saul that he would bear Christ's name before *"Gentiles and kings"* (Acts 9:15) would now, almost immediately, bring Roman proconsul Sergius Paulus to faith in Acts 13:4-12. This is the exciting dynamic of the ministry of New Testament prophets at work in the very foundational, frontier crossing stages of the church's ministry!

So, to New Testament gifts of prophecy and the New Testament prophet ...

I say 'gifts', plural, because prophecy is expressed at different levels and in different dimensions in the New Testament. Let's develop three of these: manifestation gifts, motivational gifts and ministry gifts, the latter relating to the gift of the New Testament prophet.

Manifestation Gift of Prophecy

Nine charismatic gifts are listed in I Corinthians

12:4-11, among them prophecy ...

> *"Now there are varieties of gifts, but the same Spirit; and there are varieties of service, but the same Lord; and there are varieties of activities, but it is the same God who empowers them all in everyone. To each is given the manifestation of the Spirit for the common good. For to one is given through the Spirit the utterance of wisdom, and to another the utterance of knowledge according to the same Spirit, to another faith by the same Spirit, to another gifts of healing by the one Spirit, to another the working of miracles, to another prophecy, to another the ability to distinguish between spirits, to another various kinds of tongues, to another the interpretation of tongues. All these are empowered by one and the same Spirit, who apportions to each one individually as he wills."*

The gifts here appear to be once-off expressions, which may be manifested by the Spirit's inspiration through any believer at any stage of their Christian life, in an environment of the fullness of the Holy Spirit. The expression of these gifts should not be taken as a mark of spiritual maturity or outstanding godly character, although such traits are to be longed for in every believer. Unfortunately, the church at Corinth, to whom this letter is written, despite being sadly lacking in spiritual example (I Corinthians 3:1), is also a community *"not lacking in any gift."* (I Corinthians 1:7)

It would seem from the context at Corinth that these are gifts which may be manifest through any believer during even brief moments of surrender and receptivity to the Holy Spirit. As such, they are not necessarily particular inclinations of the individuals concerned, but expressions of the will of the Spirit.

I have been in numerous meetings over many years where the Holy Spirit has impressed on one individual to share something, but they have, for whatever reason, held back. Then the Holy Spirit stirs someone else to share exactly the same thing and the original person all of a sudden can't hold their tongue, saying something like, "I had that exact same word, but I was afraid to share," or, "I thought, Maybe it's for somewhere else." The picture is very clear of the Holy Spirit, in charge of a meeting, looking for someone – anyone! – to get His message across.

The manifestation gift, in other words, doesn't belong to a person, but to the Spirit. Many of us who are familiar with the operation of these I Corinthians 12 gifts have experienced them all at different times in different situations, as the Spirit willed and the situation required, but that does not mean we have these gifts. So it is with the manifestation gift of prophecy: it can be expressed at any time through any Spirit-filled believer – that believer doesn't need to be a prophet or even have a prominent gift of prophecy, just to be filled with the Holy Spirit.

A local church environment where any and all the I Corinthians 12 gifts are welcome and expected is really healthy because, at a very basic level of operation, such a setting is dependent upon and, therefore, affirms the Holy Spirit being in charge and having complete freedom to bring out new things in new people, *"just as He wills."* It is in this free and open, yet Spirit led and controlled, context, that prominent gifting in certain individuals will begin to emerge.

Motivational Gift of Prophecy

In Romans 12:4-8, Paul lists seven charismatic gifts that have become motivational, clearly more than once-off manifestations, in certain individuals. Again, prophecy is among them ...

> *"For as in one body we have many members, and the members do not all have the same function, so we, though many, are one body*

> *in Christ, and individually members one of another. Having gifts that differ according to the grace given to us, let us use them: if prophecy, in proportion to our faith; if service, in our serving; the one who teaches, in his teaching; the one who exhorts, in his exhortation; the one who contributes, in generosity; the one who leads, with zeal; the one who does acts of mercy, with cheerfulness."*

Please note my emboldening of the words, 'have' and 'having'. In any local church where the charismatic gifts are in regular operation so many times, where it becomes particularly evident that certain individuals have a tendency to function in certain gifts. In fact, it can get to the place where can almost anticipate certain people exercising what is now clearly 'their' gift even before they open their mouths or raise their hand.

There are two key words in this passage of Scripture: gifts and graces. They are actually very similar in the original Greek: 'grace' is charis and 'gifts' are charismata. Just as charismata is a literal extension of charis, so the gifts we operate in flow out of the grace of God in our lives. So, when we talk about 'having' gifts we must be very clear that these gifts come from God, not ourselves, and are an expressing of His grace at work in our lives.

Grace, according to Peter (II Peter 3:18), is something we are to grow in and, consequently, there should be a maturing, development and enrichment of the expression of all of these gifts as we faithfully and obediently exercise them, over time. The gift of prophecy, also, is always to be consistent with the Scriptures (– remember, this is the measure against which it is to be judged by the church) and so, as an individual grows in the spiritual discipline of studying and meditating God's word, the prophetic utterances of that individual will be enriched; indeed, sometimes a prophetic utterance will consist entirely of the quotation of Scripture that is perfectly timed for that moment and person or gathering.

In Paul's Romans 12 list, there appear to be specific graces that are to be associated with each of the gifts mentioned. Just as the grace of generosity motivates the gift of giving and the grace of cheerfulness fosters the gift of mercy, so the grace of faith motivates the gift of prophecy: *"... if prophecy, in proportion to our faith."* I cannot develop my gift of prophecy beyond my growth in the grace of faith. But how do I grow in faith?

Earlier in the same letter, Paul explained that faith comes by hearing and hearing by the word of God (Romans 10:17), and so it is that as the person with the gift of prophecy spends time in God's word, listening to His voice, faith utterances – not forced or wishful thinking – will flow out of that conversation with the Father. Christians don't so much have a faith problem as a Word challenge – when we spend time abiding in God's word, the growth of faith is the outcome, and growth in the gift of prophecy, in turn, is an inevitable effect. The mature gift of prophecy is rich in the word, the will and the ways of God.

As such, the New Testament gift of prophecy should have all the traits of the word of God itself: it is an expression of the love of God (- note the embedding of the 'Love Chapter' at the heart of Paul's teaching in I Corinthians 12-14 on the operations of the gifts of the Spirit in the local church), which *"... speaks to men for edification and exhortation and comfort."* (I Corinthians 14). As surely as the word of God builds us up, encourages us and helps us grow in our faith, so the mature gift of prophecy will do this for the church.

And out from among those who grow in the gift of prophecy there will emerge prophets, leadership ministries who are not just mature in both character and gifting themselves, but graced for the maturing of the church. This brings us to the Ephesians 4 (verses 7-16) ministry gift of prophet.

Ministry Gift of Prophet

> "But to each one of us grace was given according to the measure of Christ's gift. Therefore it says, 'When He ascended on high, He led captive a host of captives, and He gave gifts to men.' (Now this expression, 'He ascended,' what does it mean except that He also had descended into the lower parts of the earth? He who descended is Himself also He who ascended far above all the heavens, so that He might fill all things.) And He gave some as apostles, and some as prophets, and some as evangelists, and some as pastors and teachers, for the equipping of the saints for the work of service (ministry), to the building up of the body of Christ; until we all attain to the unity of the faith, and of the knowledge of the Son of God, to a mature man, to the measure of the stature which belongs to the fullness of Christ. As a result, we are no longer to be children, tossed here and there by waves and carried about by every wind of doctrine, by the trickery of men, by craftiness in deceitful scheming; but speaking the truth in love, we are to grow up in all aspects into Him who is the head, even Christ, from whom the whole body, being fitted and held together by what

> *every joint supplies, according to the proper working of each individual part, causes the growth of the body for the building up of itself in love."*

Not everyone who prophesies is a prophet. In Acts 21:10, Agabus is described as a *"prophet"*. In the following verse, we read of his four daughters *"who prophesied"*, not *"prophetesses"* as is inaccurately translated in some versions. The noun, prophetai, is used of the prophets who came down from Jerusalem in Acts 11:27, but propheteuousai, the participle of the verb, literally 'prophesying ones', is used for the daughters of Agabus. (NB. This is not a gender disqualification as Anna is identified 'prophetess' in Luke 2:36.)

It is not splitting hairs to say that there is a real difference between a regular prophesier and a prophet. We should not be surprised if the children of a prophet prophesy; one of the key ministries of prophets is to release the church in the prophetic, even if most will not become prophets, in the same way as evangelists makes the church more evangelistic, and so on – how much stronger the effect within their own families?

When prophesiers are around, the church is edified, exhorted and comforted; but when prophets are around, edifiers, exhorters and comforters are raised up. This brings us to 'ascension ministries' in general, of which prophet is one.

To those who would say, for example, that there are no apostles today because an apostle had to be someone who knew Jesus in the flesh (– although such an idea collapses instantly with the apostleship of Paul himself), it should be pointed out that the Ephesians 4 gift of apostle was not released on earth until after Jesus had *"ascended on high."*

This too is the case for the prophet. The prophet is an expression of Christ the Prophet to and through the church, gifted to the body to ensure that the church rises up to the fullness of its prophetic role in the *"last days"* which, biblically, is the entire age of the New Testament church, beginning from the Day of Pentecost (See Acts 2:17a). As such, along with the other four 'headship ministries' of Ephesians 4, the prophet is a gifted, recognised leader who must be mature in the faith as one whose role it is build up the church to the collective likeness of *"a mature man."*

Prophets, as such, must exist and operate in harmonious interaction with all the other ascension ministries; the very fact that they appear second in a list of five, all of whom share a collaborative role for the equipping of the church, places them in a significantly different posture from the singled-out-and-separated nature of the Old Testament prophet. Modern day mystics, gnostics and spiritual nomads do nothing to mature the body of Christ as a prophetic people. New Testament prophets, like all ascension ministries, know how to relate to people, function in team and demonstrate accountability!

However, there is one other ascension ministry with which the prophet appears to have a particularly close and distinctive relationship: the apostle. Ephesians 2:20 says that the church is *"built on the foundation of apostles and prophets, Christ Jesus Himself being the corner stone."*

The traditional cessationist interpretation of this text has been that "apostles" here represents the New Testament and "prophets" the Old Testament. It appears a neat and tidy encapsulation of the Old and New Testament revelations as the foundation of the Christian faith – an infallible combination which Pentecostals and charismatics would never deny – but it ignores the reference to the same ministries two chapters later, within the context of all five ascension ministries.

It also ignores the examples of the role of prophets, often foundational to the recognition and releasing of ministries and the establishing of churches, found in the Book of Acts, such as the prophets from Jerusalem coming down to Antioch, the prophets in Antioch helping launch the apostolic ministry of Paul and the interaction of the prophet Agabus with the apostle Paul, all alluded to earlier in this paper. It also ignores the close partnership of apostle and prophet seen, for example, in the missionary travels of Paul and Silas.

But what is it about these ministries that make them foundational to the building and growth of the church? Clearly the foundation is not the personalities themselves: the church is not built upon the foundation which *is* apostles and prophets, but upon the foundation which is *laid* by apostles and prophets (– this misunderstanding is at the core of the Roman Catholic doctrine of apostolic succession). When Jesus told Peter, *"Upon this rock I will build My Church,"* he was not identifying Peter as our foundation, but the revelation that Peter had; namely, that Jesus is *"the Christ, the Son of the living God."* (Matthew 16:16-18)

The foundation which apostles and prophets so effectively lay together is both revelatory and directional. The prophet complements the apostle in revealing the vision and the mind of Christ in the planting, maturing and multiplying of churches, in the recognition and release of other ascension ministries; and does so in a way that opens up and applies biblical truth, with a stature and authority that is not strained, with an anointing that is unmistakeably recognised by the church, and with a humility that empowers rather than overpowers other leaders and the body around them.

God's foundational order of appointment in establishing the New Testament church is laid out in I Corinthians 12:28 ...

> "... *God has appointed in the church, first apostles, second prophets, third teachers, then miracles, then gifts of healings, helps, administrations, various kinds of tongues.*"

This order is not one of value but of function. If we must create a pyramid, it should be inverted rather than hierarchical, with apostles and prophets at the bottom rather than the top! The example of Paul clearly modelled this when he concluded, "... *God has exhibited us apostles last of all, as men condemned to death; because we have become a spectacle to the world, both to angels and to men ... the scum of all the earth ...*"! (I Corinthians 4:9, 12)

No, the order of *"first apostles, second prophets, third teachers ..."* is clearly one of process rather than of status, and it is an order that tells us two things before we even start: first, these ministries are 'first-on-site', foundational ministries which ensure that what is built will withstand the inevitable storms to follow ; and second, prophets work closer to apostles than with other ascension ministries at the earliest stages.

Printed in Great Britain
by Amazon